A Golden And Blessed Casket of Nature's Marvels

Concerning
The Blessed Mystery
Of The
PHILOSOPHER'S STONE
Containing The
REVELATION OF THE MOST ILLUMINATED EGYPTIAN
KING AND PHILOSOPHER, HERMES TRISMEGISTUS,
*Translated By Our German Hermes, The Noble Beloved Monarch
And Philosopher Trismegistus,*
A. P.H. THEOPHRASTUS PARACELSUS;
Also
TINCTURA PHYSICORUM PARACELSICA,
*With An Excellent Explanation By The
Noble and Learned Philosopher,*
ALEXANDER VON SUCHTEN, M.D.;
Together With
CERTAIN HITHERTO UNPUBLISHED TREATISES,
By This Author,
And Also Other Corollaries Of The Same Matter,
As Specified In The Preface.

*Now Published For The Use And Benefit Of All
Sons Of The Doctrine Of Hermes.*

Benedictus Figulus

ISBN 1-56459-180-8

Request our FREE CATALOG of over 1,000

Rare Esoteric Books

Unavailable Elsewhere

Alchemy, Ancient Wisdom, Astronomy, Baconian, Eastern-Thought, Egyptology, Esoteric, Freemasonry, Gnosticism, Hermetic, Magic, Metaphysics, Mysticism, Mystery Schools, Mythology, Occult, Philosophy, Psychology, Pyramids, Qabalah, Religions, Rosicrucian, Science, Spiritual, Symbolism, Tarot, Theosophy, *and many more!*

Kessinger Publishing Company
Montana, U.S.A.

CONTENTS.

	PAGE.
Preface to the English Translation ...	ix.
An Epigram concerning the Philosopher's Stone, by Alexander de S., to Gulielmus Blaucus	1
Prolocutory Dedicatory Address	3
The Book of the Revelation of Hermes, Interpreted by Theophrastus Paracelsus, concerning the Supreme Secret of the World	33
Concerning the True Medicine of the Most Distinguished Man, Alexander von Suchten	50
Man, the best and most perfect of God's creatures. A more complete Exposition of this Medical Foundation for the less Experienced Student ...	57
A Dialogue, by Alexander von Suchten, Introducing two Interlocutory Personages, viz., Alexander and Bernhardus	88
Extracts from the Book of the Three Faculties, by Alexander von Suchten	160

	PAGE
An Explanation of the Natural Philosopher's Tincture of Theophrastus Paracelsus, by Alexander von Suchten	192
Corollary concerning Hyle	259
Another Corollary, by Conrad Poyselius	260
Certain Notable Facts concerning the Philosopher's Stone	266
The Four Degrees in the Regimen of Fire	267
Concerning Salts	269
Concerning Common Salt	271
Philosophical Rules or Canons concerning the Philosopher's Stone	275
An Anonymous Treatise concerning the Philosopher's Stone	297
A Short Admonition to the Reader	325
Certain Verses of an Unknown Writer concerning the Great Work of the Tincture	327
Enigmas concerning the Tincture	334
Short Admonition to the True Hearted Reader and Son of the Doctrine	337
Concerning the Potable Gold of Theophrastus Paracelsus	339
Of the Power, Operation, and exceedingly beneficial Use of the Glorious Antidote termed Potable Gold	343
Index	358

PREFACE TO THE ENGLISH TRANSLATION.

NO investigation seems likely to elucidate the obscurity which envelops the life of the strange alchemist who called himself Benedictus Figulus, and is otherwise distinguished as poet, theologian, theosopher, philosopher, physician, and, more curiously still, as eremite of Utenhofen and Hagenau. The second term of his assumed appellation signifies a potter, and it has been conjectured accordingly that his real name was Törpffer. There are no biographical data forthcoming in support of this or any other assumption. He comes before us as a very ardent and devout disciple of Theophrastus Paracelsus, bent on collecting his works, to redeem them from destruction on the one hand, and from mutilation and perversion on the other.

As a purely original writer he does not seem to have accomplished anything of special importance either for alchemy or literature. "The Golden and Blessed Casket of Nature's Marvels," which is the most interesting of all his works, and is here presented for the first time to the English reader, is an ingarnering of a friend's manuscripts. So also with the other publications of this author—he is an editor, commentator, and translator, rather than a creative writer. That he had aspirations above these humble but useful duties, is exhibited in his interesting prolocutory discourse, which introduces the present collection, and provides us at the same time with a certain measure of insight into his own early history and struggles. The distinction which he desired to attain was, however, denied him, even within the somewhat contracted sphere of mystic possibility, for, in his obscurity, he has been actually overlooked by the keen eye of the chief bibliographer of alchemy, Lenglet du Fresnoy.

The works of Benedictus Figulus which are known to the present writer, are as follows:—

The Heavenly Tripartite Golden Treasury: That is — a heavenly and golden treasure of many choice rarities, wherein lies concealed the ancient, blessed, and great Carbuncle and Treasure. Divided into three parts.

I. The Magic Secret of D. Philippus Theophrastus Paracelsus; also of Bernard, Count of the March; and the Apostles' Creed cabalistically elucidated. Also Fr. Vincentius Koffsckius, Concerning the First Vegetable Tincture and the First Matter.

II. The Hermetic School, wherein may be learned the preparation of the royal, oriental, transparent Ruby of the blessed Astral Magnet of the Magical and Chaldean Tinging Stone.

III. The Light Shining in the Darkness, of Raymond Lully, being an aid to investigate the highest Secret of Nature, and to educe it from concealment into light, according to the philosophical usage. How also to prepare the Blessed Stone of the Philosophers, with the secret of philosophically augmenting it in virtue.

Now dedicated, presented, and published to all Lovers of Divine Truth and of Hermetic Philosophy, and to all Sons of the Doctrine, who seek the root of the high magical Tincture, and are lovers of the heavenly, dear, and noble Art of Alchemy. By Benedictus Figulus, of Utenhofen, etc., etc. Frankfort, 1608. 4to.

The New Olympic and Blessed Rosary: That is—a fresh, living, philosophical Garland of Roses. In two parts.

Part I. Shewing from King Solomon the Wise, H. Solomon Trismosinus, H. Trithemius, and Dom. Theophrastus, how the Blessed Golden Bough and Treasured

Tincture are to be obtained from the everlasting, oriental Tree of the Hesperides, by means of the Grace of God. A faithful revelation to every individual Son of the Hermetic Doctrine, and Lover of the Teaching of D. Theophrastus.

Part II. Containing a book, with thirty-two chapters, of Laurentius Venturus Venetus, Doctor of Medicine, etc., On the Blessed Stone of the Philosophers. Faithfully translated, for the first time, from the Latin into the German tongue. By Benedictus Figulus, of Utenhofen, etc., etc. Printed at the cost of the Author. Basle, 1608. 4to.

Hortulus Olympicus Aureolus: That is —a Heavenly, Golden, Hermetic Pleasure Garden, planted by old and new Philosophers, giving an instruction for the disintegration of the celestial, noble, highly blessed, sulphur-red and scarlet-blue of the exceedingly brilliant and tinging Carbuncle Stone, whereby human, vegetable, and metallic bodies may attain their renovation and highest perfection, or completeness. Now presented and issued to all the Sons of the Doctrine, by Benedictus Figulus, of Utenhofen, etc., etc. Printed at Frankfort-on-the-Maine, by Wolfgang Richter, at the cost of Nicolaus Steinius. 1608. 4to.

The Golden Hermetic Paradise, flowing with Nectar and Ambrosia, by carefully, faithfully, and visually investigating which, we may learn how the Golden Apples of the Hesperides may be plucked from the Philosophical Tree. Hitherto concealed, but now unlocked and manifested for the benefit and profit of the Sons of the Chemico-Spagyric Doctrine. By Benedictus Figulus, of Utenhofen, etc., etc. Printed at Frankfort, by Wolfgang Richter, at the cost of Nicolaus Steinius. 1608. 4to.

In addition to these, there are several less important works, by writers now forgotten, with which Figulus was editorially connected, but these it is unnecessary to enumerate, as they are not concerned with Alchemy. Finally, there is the "Pandora," or "Golden Casket," which is now offered to the reader. These writings are all exceedingly scarce, and, concerning their author, it only remains to be added that his name has been cited as a witness to the existence of secret Hermetic societies anterior to the appearance of the first Rosicrucian manifesto, the *Fama Faternitatis*. It is fairly well known, even outside the strict limits of informed Hermetic criticism, that the Brotherhood of the Rose and the Cross has claimed, in its official publications, an antiquity which historical evidence is not in a position to corroborate. As Figulus preceded by a few years the accepted dates of those documents which originally revealed the existence of such an association, considerable interest must naturally attach to his statement that there was a secret society of alchemists so far back as the year 1607, which connected with the brotherhood mentioned by Raymund Lully, as established in Italy at the beginning of the fifteenth century, and merged at the date mentioned in the association supposed to have been founded by the mysterious Christian Rosencrantz.

Benedictus Figulus belonged to the Catholic school of Alchemy; and herein, as in other matters, he differed widely from the college of initiation, which was typified by the Rose and the Cross. He has left us, indeed, in one of his collections, a most curious exemplar of a Hermetic Mass, containing variations in the Introit, Collects, Antiphons, and other portions of the Ordinary, which are outwardly invocations for the gift of Divine Illumination upon the secrets of "philosophy," but inwardly would appear to contain an arcane instruction. With these may be profitably compared the Mass for the soul of an Alchemist, printed at a later date in certain Hermetic Museums. There is no conclusive reason for supposing that Figulus had attained to the Great Mystery of adeptship. He was, however, an ardent seeker, sufficiently equipped to regard his ultimate success with some confidence. Thus we find him ("Prolocutory and Dedicatory Speech," page 29 of this volume) guaranteeing to reward those who would assist him in the recovery of Paracelsian manuscripts with a grateful compensation "when we (D.V.) shortly reach our goal in philosophy and medicine." On the whole, Benedictus Figulus, although admittedly a minor figure, is one which should not be overlooked in the history of mystical transmutation, and he is additionally interesting by reason of his fervent and even religious devotion to the Art and its accepted Masters.

Alexander von Suchten, with whose writings we are mainly concerned in the "Golden and Blessed Casket," comes before us under another light, that is, as an initiated proficient in that school wherein Figulus was only graduating. His life, like that of his editor, is involved in as much mystery as the Grand Arcanum itself, and he also, in the Dialogue between Alexander and Bernhardus, may perhaps be regarded as affording us a few indirect gleams of personal information.

When the works of this curious and aspirational philosopher first became known to the present editor, through the careful and loving labours of Figulus, a very absorbing possibility was at once opened up, and one also which it is still worth while to glance at, so that future investigators of the thorny byways of esoteric literature may be spared at least one trap. The *Novum Lumen Chemicum*, which has recently become available to English readers among the treatises of "The Hermetic Museum," is well known to all students of the subject as a classic of Alchemy. It is equally well known that Michael Sendivogius, the disciple of Alexander Seton, claimed it as his own composition, and did, in fact and for a long time, enjoy the reputation of a first-grade adept on account of it. The mendacious character of this claim has, however, been sufficiently established, and there is little doubt that it was really the work of his master, or that Sendivogius did nothing but mutilate it. The chief evidence for these statements will be found in the *Lettre de Desnoyers*, secretary of the Princess Mary of Gonzagon, Queen of Poland – in the "Alchemical Anecdotes" of Guldenfalk, in Georg Morhof's *Epistola de Metallorum Transmutatione*, and in Theobald de Hogheland. It was collected by Louis Figuier in *L'Alchimie et Les Alchimistes*, and has been further resumed in the "Lives of Alchemystical Philosophers," enlarged from the original edition, and published in 1887.

Now, just as the *Novum Lumen Chemicum* is conspicuous among alchemical writings for its precision and clearness, as well as for a certain savour of inspiration and genius, which are wanting in much of this literature, so is its true author conspicuous in the college of adepts. While he is illustrious by reason of his transmutations, he is hallowed by the misfortunes of his history. He is the chief, and, to some extent, the one martyr of Alchemy, who, at the hands of the Elector of Saxony, suffered innumerable tortures, "was pierced with pointed iron, scorched with molten lead, burnt by fire, beaten with rods, racked from head to foot," and wasted by solitary confinement, rather than betray his secret. His deliverance was at length effected, but his sufferings resulted in his death, which took place in the year 1604. Now, Alexander Seton was a Scotchman, very evidently belonging to the ancient and noble house of that name, but his early life is unknown. When he undertook the Hermetic propaganda which closed so tragically at Dresden, he assumed various disguises, and adopted various names, while that which he actually bore has been the subject of numerous variations—Sethon, Sidon, Sethonius, Scotus, Sitonius, Sidonius, Suthoneus, Suethonius, and even Seehthonius, are enumerated by Louis Figuier, and when we find flourishing at that period, and dying apparently about the same time, a certain Alexander von Suchten, otherwise unknown, it is anything but *prima facie* improbable that this was another variant of the much perverted name of Alexander Seton, or that Benedictus Figulus was, like Michael Sendivogius, the literary heir and executor of the great master. There are many small coincidental points which would help to support the presumption, as, for example, that both of them were apparently Catholics at a period when the Catholic faith was professed by few in Scotland, and it is altogether needless to inform the Hermetic reader that could the identity be established a great and lasting interest would attach to the contents of the "Golden Casket" for all those who, practically or philosophically, take any interest in alchemical literature.

A searching inquiry has, however, failed to establish the conjecture on any reasonable ground; the posthumous fragments of Alexander von Suchten are fairly conclusive as to his German nationality; it is certain that he was publishing at Basle so early as the year 1573, long before the appearance of Seton; and, finally, in the year 1608, we find Benedictus Figulus interpreting into German the Dialogue between Mercury, the Alchemist, and Nature,* which forms part of the *Novum Lumen*, without any elucidation of its true authorship, but, on the contrary, accepting the authorship of Sendivogius, for he permits the anagram containing the name of the pseudo-Polish pretender to pass unchallenged on his title-page.

Beyond the posthumous treatises in the "Golden Casket," Suchten is credited as follows:—

---

* The German translation in question begins on page 96 of *Thesaurinella Aurea Tripartita*. There is also a reproduction of the Latin original in *Paradisus Aureolus Hermeticus*.

Mysteria Antimonii, 8vo, Basle, 1573.
The Same, in German, Nuremberg, 1613.
De Secretis Antimonii Liber, translated from the German into the Latin tongue, 8vo, Basle, 1575.
Another Edition, 8vo, London, 1670.
Clavis Alchimiæ, together with the treatise on Antimony. Both in German, 8vo, Montisbelligardi, 1614.

This enumeration rests upon the authority of Lenglet du Fresnoy; the works themselves would appear to be practically *introuvable;* at any rate there is no library in Great Britain which contains a single exemplar.

Scattered through the other writings and compilations of Figulus there are various reverential references to Alexander von Suchten, but only on one occasion do we find a considerable citation. This is from the forgotten treatise on Antimony, and in view of its rarity, it seems worth while to reproduce it.

Certain Excellent Questions on Antimony and its Composition.

By Alexander von Suchten.

What is Antimony?—It is a mineral divinely created from a metallic matter, that is, from argent vive, cooked with sulphur in the bowels of the earth.

Since metals are also produced from Mercury and Sulphur, are they and Antimony the same thing?—The argent vive of Antimony and of the metals is altogether one thing and one matter. But seeing that as to its form the Sulphur of Antimony is not metallic but mineral, and at the same time is such a Sulphur as can be altered by digestion, and can arrive at a purity impossible in the case of the Sulphur of other metals, Antimony is an imperfect metal, and is called Saturn in philosophy.

What is to be expected from Antimony?—The Highest Medicine, the like of which the world cannot produce, and that also which the Wise have sought from the commencement of the world.

How is this obtained?—By great toil and labour, but, before all, by the Grace of God.

What is the method of procedure?—First, a Mercury must be separated on the white, even as the miner separates Antimony from the ore in which it has grown, yet with the precaution that the metallic brilliance visible in Antimony shall be neither burnt nor removed by fire, but shall come out more exalted and better. Moreover, this metallic form must remain even on the whiteness of the silver. Then is it in its highest degree, but as soon as the slag whence it comes disappears, it is no longer Antimony but the Mercury of the Philosophers, and is fusible like any other metal. In flux it is even as a clear quicksilver.

What is the great importance of the brilliance?—The metallic form is a living fire which accomplishes all that is effected in this work, even to the end of the digestion, and this fire is its life, whereby the matter containing it is purified from all uncleanness. The same fire, moreover, is the life and matter of all metals. When the form departs, they cease to live.

What escapes in the separation which might be injurious?—The humours and earthly sulphur of the other mineral bodies which augment the poison of the Mercury.

What then is Mercury?—It is nothing else than an argent vive which cleaves to mineral Sulphur, while the latter is a pure Sulphur, albeit red and imperfect. When digested and reduced to its perfection, it becomes the Arcanum, the argent vive tinged and transmuted from a poisonous state into the noblest Medicine. On this point the student should diligently examine our *Philosophia Mysteria Præmia von Antimonio*, and the *Triumphal Chariot* of Basil Valentine. Failure will only result through the withholding of Divine Favour.

In the several treatises which make up the "Golden Casket" there are a variety of points which will instruct as well as interest the modern student of the esoteric philosophies. Much that has been recently advanced as a novel presentation of so-called secret doctrine, and, in this sense, as news from the invisible world now for the first time made public, will be found to have been already stated, with reasonable perspicuity, by Alexander von Suchten, while from the ethical and spiritual standpoint the mystical teaching of this old German adept will not infrequently compare with any later sources of arcane illumination.

The separation at death of the three chief constituent principles of man—that doctrine which under one or other form has been lately so much paraded—will be found upon page 17 of the present volume, and with it a short but suggestive prelection concerning that highest factor which is called "the Spirit of the Image," which returns to Him by Whom the image was impressed, and in which image we must live if we would attain true wisdom. The concentration of consciousness in the highest principle is here plainly inculcated, as it is again in the doctrine concerning the Iliastic and Necrocosmic Heaven (page 24), "out of which the soul has never come," and into the consciousness of which we must all rise in order to achieve ourselves. Curious and interesting also is the speculation concerning the "spiritual magnet" which attracts the eternal sapience.

The chief secret of the medical philosophy, derived by Alexander von Suchten from his master Paracelsus, would appear to consist in the application of the "soul of the world" to the universal healing of humanity. The prescriptions of the exoteric pharmacy are in themselves useless; herbs have no real virtue, but they are the signs of the true medicine for physical necessity, after the same manner that Church ordinances direct us to that fountain wherein is man's spiritual healing, but are not themselves the fountain. This singular instruction concerning symbolical medicine will be found at page 181. The soul of the world, which is the source of all riches as well as of bodily prosperity, is identified with the Spirit of Truth that the world cannot comprehend without revelation or initiation (page 37). It is also the Spirit of God, but this term is to be interpreted rather as the Divine Breath, or the Divine Activity, than in the higher sense which usually attaches to it (page 43). It is the sovereign force as distinguished from the sovereign intelligence, and its special centres would appear to be the Sun and Moon of the Macrocosm, to which correspond the interior Sol and Luna of the lesser or microcosmic world (page 52). At the same time, this secret essence is elsewhere (page 168) identified with the Mystery of the Incarnation, the opening of Heaven to St. Stephen, and the ecstatic rapture of St. Paul.

The commentary of Alexander von Suchten on the Tincture of Natural Philosophy, being a treatise of Theophrastus Paracelsus, is, in the absence of the work upon Antimony, the chief available source of information concerning the chemical philosophy of Suchten, and it will be found to reproduce a tradition, already practically universal in Alchemy, that the processes of the *Magnum opus* are strictly analagous to those which are attributed by Genesis to the creation of the greater world. Thus, the confection of the Philosophical Stone is the creation of a *minutum mundum*, and has, therefore, further, an equally strict analogy with the microcosmus of man. Whatever value may attach to these mystical parallels, Suchten appears to have possessed a clear and liberal mind, which penetrated the letter of the mystics, and could grasp the interior significance. He had transcended, for example, the mere exoteric belief in the astrological operation of the sidereal forces. "The Sun and Moon I see above me influence me neither for good nor bad, but the Sun and Moon and Planets, with which God's providence has adorned the Heaven in me, which also is the seat of the Almighty, these have the power to rule and reform me according to their course ordained by God" (page 185).

Taken altogether, there is much in this little volume which will be rightly regarded as of moment during the present revived interest in Hermetic wisdom.

ARTHUR EDWARD WAITE.

An Epigram concerning the Philosopher's Stone.

BY
Alex. de S., to Gulielmus Blancus.

We dissolve the living body with Apollo's fire—

So that what was before a Stone may become a Spirit.

From the inmost parts of this we extract Gold,

Which, with natal seed, cleanses impure ores from the dross of their mother.

After we have separated the bones, these kindred we then wash with water

From them is born a Bird, arrayed in various colours, and, being made white, it flies into the air.

So we with new fire paint its wings, and, being coloured, imbue them with its milk:

As for the rest, we feed it with Blood,

Until, full grown, it may bear the fury of Mulciber (*i.e.*, Vulcan=fire).

This Bird, O Gulielmus! the Thrice Great Hermes called his own,

And the whole world has not its like.

O Christ, graciously grant that this blessed long-desired bird be born in our Garden!

PROLOCUTORY, DEDICATORY ADDRESS

TO

THE WORSHIPFUL, NOBLE, ETC., ETC.,

MASTER MICHAEL DANIEL PLEICKHARD,

SURNAMED POLAND, OF THE HIGH AND
REVEREND CATHEDRAL CHAPTER
AT STRASBURG, COUNCILLOR;

AND TO

THE HONOURED, LEARNED, ETC., ETC.,

MASTER BALTHAZAR KEYBEN,

I.V. DOCTOR,

IN FRANKFORT-ON-THE-MAIN;

AS ALSO TO

THE HONOURED, MOST EXPERIENCED, ETC., ETC.,

MASTER JOHN ENOCH MEYER,

MASTER BUILDER OF THE CITY OF STRASBURG,
AND STEWARD OF THE CONVENT OF
ST. NICHOLAS IN UNDIS, IN
THAT ILK;

HIS GENEROUS, WELL-BELOVED MASTERS
AND BENEFICENT PATRONS.

HERE FOLLOWS THE

PROLOCUTORY, DEDICATORY SPEECH.

———

WORSHIPFUL, Noble, etc., generous Masters and Patrons, when reviewing the whole course of my studies, from my youth up, I find—and have indeed hitherto found in my work, and clearly experienced more and more with the lapse of time, as daily experience shews is wont ~~to~~ happen to the true believer and right naturalist—that there are three kinds of Philosophy or Wisdom, of which the world partly makes use, some more than others, some of this and others of that. Yet one of these Three alone is Eternal, Indestructible, and may stand before God Almighty (of which, however, but few students are found), because it proceeds and flows from above from the Father of Light. Now, the First is the Common Philosophy of Aristotle, of Plato, and of our own time, which is but a Cagastrian Philosophy, Speculation, and Phantasy, with which, even at the present day, all the Schools are filled, and by which they are befooled, and beloved youth thereby led astray. The same is inane, erroneous, empty chatter; and far removed from the foundation of Truth. Even at the present day it is blasphemously defended, tooth and nail, with all sorts of opinions, ideas, imaginations, and erroneous thoughts of the old heathen (who were held to be Sages), which were accepted as the Truth. For it is derived from an unpropitious Heaven and Stars, evil Influences, also Inspirations of Satan, and at that time was considered a great Mystery and Sacred Thing, as it also is at this present by the great majority of learned men. But this is an erroneous, false, fatal, misleading sophistry, which, like the body in the grave, is brought to nought but dust and ashes, and is the same against which the inspired Apostle Paul warns us in his Epistle: "Beware of vain philosophy," and "Beware lest any man spoil you through philosophy and vain deceit."

This Philosophy, although, from my youth up, it was earnestly and diligently inculcated, and forced upon me, in the Schools (as unfortunately occurs to others at the present day), yet, by special interposition of the Holy Spirit, it became so suspected by me that I never would, nor could, torture my head, mind, and soul with it, nor persuade my heart that the same was a sacred thing, nor cleave unto it as others did; but, according to my childish judgment, let the matter rest there until, about the year 1587 or 1588, another philosophy came into my hands. At the same time I had, in my own mind, firmly resolved not to remain the least among my fellow scholars, but in due time to graduate in advance of all.

But it has pleased God otherwise in His Divine Providence, and all sorts of impediments on the part of my superiors hindered the course of my studies, until at last, in 1587-88, the books and writings of Theophrastus, of Roger Bacon, and of M. Isaac the Hollander, fell into my hands; in which I, especially in medicine (for they wrote about the Universal Stone and Medicine), saw and found a better foundation, and yet understood it not at first. But I took such a liking to the subject that I resolved not to die. nor yet to take my ease, until I had obtained this Universal Stone and Blessed Heavenly Medicine. However, the poverty of my parents and the impossibility of obtaining the necessary funds (for at that time but few princes and nobles patronised this study) compelled me unwillingly to relinquish my plan, although I was so eager for it that, for many months, I could not sleep on account of it. At last, in 1590, I found myself plunged by the devil and his friends into great misery, misfortune, and sickness, out of which God mercifully helped me when my death would have been preferred to my recovery, and when, from reasons of poverty, I had been held to commerce against my will, by my relatives, suffering all manner of persecution, partly from the Anti-Christian mob, partly from false brethren, wife, and friends, tortured, plagued, and agitated, and thus thoroughly tried by the devil. But having been rescued from the same by God's fatherly care, I turned my attention for some years to poetry, whereunto, when I found that it was irksome to all, I said good-bye; and, only three years ago, I returned to this true Philosophy, the Study of Medicine and the Theophrastic School – for which God be praised—and have publicly declared myself a disciple of Paracelsus. From this neither the devil nor the world, with its serpents and viper brood, shall, or can, ever turn me away.

The other philosophy can never teach us the "know thyself," nor the foundation of Natural Revelation, in which some heathen philosophers, particularly Pythagoras, had progressed so far that they might with reason be preferred to many professed Christians of to-day. He especially from the stars and the creatures of this earth learnt more about Nature than our arrogant, boasting philosophers, who, at bottom, understanding nothing themselves, would fain teach others.

But this our Hermetic Philosophy, which comprises the true Astronomy, Alchemy, and Magic, as also Cabala, etc., is an extremely ancient, true, Natural Science, derived from Adam, who, both before and after the Fall, had full knowledge of all things, and handed it down from father to son through the partriarchs and dear friends of God. After the Flood the general understanding and knowledge of this true natural philosophy became weakened in force and scattered in fragments in all directions; hence arose a subdividing of the whole into parts—and one has become an Astronomer, another a Magician, a third a Cabalist, a fourth an Alchemist, and especially did it afterwards flourish in Egypt. For instance, the smith, Abraham Tubalkaim, past master in all kinds of brass and iron work, and also an excellent Astrologer and Arithmetician, brought these arts with him from Egypt into the Land of Canaan. And the great skill, wisdom, and knowledge in the above arts attained by the Egyptians was by them also communicated to other nations.

The Chaldeans, Hebrews, Persians, Egyptians, have also always possessed and cultivated this knowledge, together with Theology and instruction in Divine things. Thus, Moses was so informed by all good arts in the schools of the Egyptians that he became perfect in wisdom, and therefore was not in vain chosen by God to be the leader of the people of Israel.

Thus also Daniel, from his youth up, learnt and imbibed this art in the Schools of the Chaldeans, as his Prophecies, and his skill in all kinds of interpretation before King Nebuchadnezzar and King Belshazzar, clearly and wondrously testify. Such Philosophers and Magi were also the Three Wise Men from the East, who sought Christ Jesus from the Rising of the Sun, and found him in a manger at Bethlehem.

But subsequent to the origin of this Divine Magic and natural true Philosophy, namely, 27 years after the Flood—about the year 1680, A.M.—among the Chaldeans, Persians, and afterwards in Egypt, the idolatrous and superstitious Greeks, having heard of the same, their noblest and sagest men proceeded to Chaldea and Egypt, in order that they might learn such wisdom in their Schools. But they did not relish the teaching of God's word from the Holy Bible and the Law of Moses, and, depending upon their reason and understanding, wished to be cleverer and wiser than God Himself, as is the wont of Lucifer and his disciples; for it always happens that where God builds a Church, the devil sets his chapel up beside it;

as is also recorded in the New Testament, for when Christ, the greatest Spagyric Philosopher and Heavenly Sower, sowed His good seed, the Enemy immediately threw his tares and weeds upon it, which, alas, happens to this day. Therefore have they fallen away from the foundation and essence of all Natural Mysteries and hidden Arts, and have sought wisdom in the senseless, stupid, erroneous, and deceptive Star of Satan, with which they have obscured and diluted the truth. For their own pride and presumption have hindered, befooled, and plunged them into error. For, after having learnt a little from the Chaldeans and Egyptians, they became so puffed up and proud, depending more than was meet on their own understanding, that they began to criticise things with many false and vain inventions, and took upon themselves to ascribe them to a false philosophy, concocted in their own subtle brains, under the influence of that evil star; which false philosophy not only got the upperhand among the

Greeks, but spread from them to the Latins, who, not less than the former, also wished to shew their own understanding immediately they had acquired a little knowledge, whence, instead of improving, increasing, or adorning, they have only made things worse.

Now, by these this so-called Philosophy has been disseminated throughout entire Europe. Almost all Academies and High Schools teach it, to the neglect of Moses and the Prophets, even of Christ Himself not only in Germany, but in almost all other nations. When anyone advances aught of the true Philosophy, grounded in the Word of God, but which is contrary to theirs, he is not only contemned, mocked, and laughed at, but is called an eccentric, a heretic, and haeresiarch—as has happened to me at the hands of certain pseudo-levites—or is even persecuted. The old proverb remains true: "The world wishes to be deceived." Satan is a clever juggler, using many deceptions with which he leads astray all Christendom, shewing the way unto the eternal night of hell with his dark lantern, which they take to be a true guiding light. Let him who would be deceived continue in his present course; on a certain day he will find, with eternal lamentations, howling, and gnashing of teeth, how hot hell is.

But, generous Masters and Friends, if we would follow after the true Natural Philosophy, founded on the Light of Nature; if we would acquire the same as our Spagyric Philosophy, true Astronomy, and Magic, where and under whom shall we study this? Shall we seek the teachers and professors in the Universities? Verily, we shall not find it there, for they are the true enemies, mockers, and persecutors of our Philosophy, and of all its adherents. "Art has no haters but the ignorant." They would rather remain with the husks and chaff, which the wind strews hither and thither, than with the good nourishing grain, rye, and wheat from the great store-houses or treasury of the Eternal

God and Bountiful Lord, which He gives, and invites us to partake of Where then, I ask, shall we seek it, and in what school? Dear Masters and Friends, we neither can, nor should, nor must look for it elsewhere than in the Stars; there is the school from which everything is learned.

All Natural Art and Wisdom are given by the Stars to men, and we are the disciples of the Stars. The Constellations are our natural teachers. From the light of Nature we must learn as from our father from whom we are made and begotten. The Stars are our lawful instructors, for all understanding and Art come to us from them. God has so ordered it that the natural light is in the Stars, and in the same has He laid the treasure of men to be obtained from them. But what man learns from the stars is all temporal knowledge, reason, art; what also is of the light of Nature must be derived from the same source. In short, the firmament teaches us whatsoever pertains to things temporal. But that which pertains to the immortal soul, and to the godly conversation of the inner man, all that must be learned from God. For it concerns the Image of God, and it is the office of the Holy Spirit to instruct men in things eternal.

Now, there are two bodies in man, one formed from the elements, and the other from the stars. Through death the elementary body, with its spirit, is brought to the grave, and the ethereal body and spirit are consumed in their firmament. But the spirit of the Image goes to Him in whose image it is. Thus each one dies in that of which he is, and is buried in the same. Thus, also, does death divide from each other the three spirits of man. Therefore, the wise man is he who lives in the wisdom given him by God; lives in the image of the Lord, the same ruling over his planetary and elementary body. But, brethren, man should walk, as regards his earthly body, according to the law of Nature, as did the old heathen Sages; and, for the rest, in the Will of God and the Holy

Spirit, and not set the mortal body with its wisdom above the Immortal Image (as almost all the world now does, with its fancied, spurious wisdom). Neither should he reject the Eternal Image for the animal body in his fancied wisdom, wherefore the Lord Jesus has not said in vain in His Gospel concerning the tax penny: "Render unto Cæsar the things that are Cæsar's, and unto God the things that are God's." What did He mean to convey by that? Why this, that the body, according to the natural life, belongs to Cæsar, and shall be subject to him as to its earthly head upon earth. But the soul belongs to God, and the same shall be given again to God, and shall make answer for its work. That is, he shall return Him His Image according to the spiritual life, as to his Heavenly Lord, from whom body and soul each separately come. Therefore he shall walk in His laws according to the Will of God, that he may return to God His Image, and the eternal fiery breath of life entrusted him, as it were, shall be given into Abraham's bosom, and not be cast out from before His Face eternally into outermost darkness on account of godless, devilish life and conversation. Such was Christ's meaning and object. Now he who lives according to the Image of the Lord, overcomes the stars, and should with reason be considered a wise man, although by a blind and senseless world he may be held as a fool.

But to philosophise farther concerning these things belongs not in this place to mortal philosophy, but to the Eternal, Immortal wisdom, which we have alluded to, which has Christ Jesus as its Founder, concerning whom we have the voice of the Father, saying: "Hear ye him"; so also His own voice calls to us (Matthew xi.): "Come unto Me all ye who are heavy laden. . . . . Learn from Me, for I am meek and lowly in heart," etc. From Him must we derive the Heavenly and Eternal Philosophy in order that we may come to the

Kingdom of Heaven. Of the above Philosophy we will, D.V., treat briefly elsewhere. But in this place we must consider somewhat more at length the Mortal and Natural Philosophy. For I am, and will remain to my grave, the fervent disciple and follower of the Natural and Mortal, and the Supernatural Heavenly Instruction, having totally repudiated the false, heathen wisdom which proceeds not from the true light and groundwork of Nature, since beside Christ and His Wisdom there is in the world only vanity of vanities. But to return to our intention of exploring Nature. Generous Masters and Friends, this cannot be done by sitting at the fireside nor by poring over philosophical tomes. No, if we would explore Nature in our Philosophy, and attain the desired successful results, we must tread the books of Nature with our feet. Writings are examined by means of letters, but Nature by going from land to land. In this way one finds occasionally pious and faithful Nicodemuses, Naturalists,

Philosophers, Explorers of Nature, and Lovers of our Spagyric Philosophy (I speak not now of the knavish, vagabond, false Alchemists, on whose account I would not move a step). From such as these, in addition to one's own observations, one can often obtain much useful knowledge. Hence each fresh country is a new leaf in the Book of Nature. Thus is our *Codex Naturæ* sufficiently large and ample, the leaves of which must be turned over with our feet, and examined with the spirit of understanding, and, although we be called vagabonds and land loupers by the big wigged doctors and syrup boilers, that matters nothing to me. The disciple should not fare better than his master, and the same thing has happened to Theophrastus, our dear Preceptor and Monarch of Arts, also to Alex. von Suchten, Phœdro, and others. Therefore, on my journeys I regard but little what is made by men's hands though others think much of it, but the works of God alone, these I regard, admire, and seek to explore. To find out their three principles, to separate the pure from the impure, and thereby, to the praise and glory of God, to benefit myself and my neighbours in body and soul, is my highest endeavour. For all created things are living letters and books in which can be deciphered the origin of man, in which also may be read what man is. Before all things, let everyone commend to himself the *Nosce teipsum*, that he may know himself, as Aristotle said to Alexander the Great: " Know thyself and thou shalt possess all things"; and Morienus: " those who do in themselves hold all things, are in need of no other aid."

Therefore also am I content with these three books, from which I may learn very wisdom.

The first is the great, full-meaning Book of Nature, written not with ink or stylus, but by the finger of God, wherein, lying open before our eyes, are inscribed and registered Heaven, Earth, and all creatures therein, through the sacred impress of the Three in One—which volume is called Macrocosmus.

The second is the Small Book, which with all its leaves and pieces is taken from the larger work, and this is Man himself, for whose sake all that God has ever created is there; the same also is called Microcosmus. And man alone is the instrument of Natural Light, to fulfil and shew by arts and wisdom what God has ordered in the firmament. Also He has further ordered that man have a twofold magnet—*viz.*, one composed of three elements (his body), and hence also he attracts them to himself— another of the stars, by which he attracts from the stars the Microcosmic tense. Therefore, the Reason of man has a magnet which attracts into itself the mind and thoughts of the Stars. From these, I say, yet another arises in the true believers, Magi, and Cabalists, and this third magnet is hidden in the image of God, in man's soul. The same penetrates, through faith, to Him from whom it came, and seeks eternal wisdom from the Holy Ghost, promised by Christ to it. It must be well remembered that there are two souls in man, the Eternal and the Natural, that is, two lives. One is subject to death, the other resists death. Thus also there are two souls, the Eternal and the Natural,—the Natural soul is in the starry body, and the starry body in the fleshly one, and these two together form one man but two bodies.

There are also two heavens in man, the one is *Luna Cerebrum*, the Cagastrian heaven. But in the heart of man is the true Iliastic, Necrocosmic heaven. Yes, the heart of man itself is the true heaven of Immortal being, out of which the Soul has never yet come, which New Olympus and Heaven Christ Jesus has chosen for a dwelling in all true believers. The third Book is the Holy Bible, the Holy Writ of the Old and New Testaments, which explains to us the two preceding Books. The Divine Chronicles, inspired by the Holy Ghost, shew how the Great World was created for the

Small World (Man), who in the great world is fed, nourished, and preserved by God the Father. The same, after the Fall, was by God's Son delivered from everlasting punishment, who also has been born again through water and the Spirit, is fed with the Heavenly Manna and Immortal Food of the New Creature, and is guided by the Holy Ghost to the knowledge of all Truth.

Generous Masters and Friends, from these three Books we can, by the Grace of God and the Holy Spirit, learn that which will profit us in body and soul for Time and Eternity, and avoid all heathenish deceitful books, of which the world is full.

But to return to our occult Hermetic Philosophy: Beloved Masters and Friends, we, with others, have to complain not a little that, although innumerable devilish philosophers have written about the Universal Medicine and the Philosopher's Stone, yet both Heathens and Christians have left us true writings, which godless Cacosophists and pseudo-sophists have, for the most part, either wholly kept back or altered.

Truly this is a trick of the devil, that his jugglery and lies, with which he for many centuries dazzled and befooled the world, may not be brought to light.

We have further to complain of those who mutilate and falsify the works of true seekers after Natural Wisdom and Art, for I have clearly discovered defects, alterations, and foreign matter in the "Triumphal Chariot" of Fr. Basilius, and also in the writings of A. von Suchten and Theophrastus. More especially, dear Friends, have we to complain of the devilish cunning way in which the works of Theophrastus have hitherto been suppressed, only a few of which (and those to be reckoned the very worst) having appeared in print. For although they have been collected together from all countries in which Theophrastus has lived and travelled—the books he has written in Astronomy, Philosophy, Chemistry, Cabala, and Theology, numbering some thousand volumes—yet the same has only been done from avarice to get riches. For, having been trafficked in and sold for great sums, they have become scattered among the courts of princes and nobles, while Christendom at large, for whose use and benefit Theophrastus wrote, has no part in them. Particularly his theological works (because they annihilate the godless, and do not suit children of this world—belly-servers, deceived by the devil), have hitherto been totally suppressed. For which devilish end Thurneyser, a true instrument of Satan, who with his lies and false Alchemy has cheated all the world, Electors and Princes, great and small, has (amongst others whom I will here spare) been made great use of.

But, at the Last Day, before the Judgment Seat of Christ, I, together with all true sons of the Doctrine, shall demand an account of them for having stolen, sold, divided, and shut Truth away in boxes, walls, and vaults, and behind locks and bolts. Now, these precious and revered writings were ordered by God in our latter times, through Theophrastus, for the use and weal of the whole of Christendom. As regards our dear, highly-favoured Monarch and Preceptor, Ph. Theophrastus, of blessed memory, we, for our part, will not suppress his Life, his well-merited praise, and his immortal fame, given him by God, the Angels, and the whole Firmament, but will heartily defend his honour and teaching to the very end our life. Therefore (D.V.), we shall shortly endeavour to promote the same in an especial manner by publishing, to begin with, his Cabalistic and Theological Books, for the weal and salvation of Christendom, in order that the three-headed Antichrist, or three unclean spirits in the Apocalypse, may be right well recognised and avoided by all. Being therefore resolved, with the aid of Christ, to publish as many of Theophrastus' works as can be got together, I shall do so in the comforting assurance and hope of cordial assistance and support from all zealous, Christian lovers and followers of the true and Christian Philosophy, derived from our Heavenly Philosopher, Christ Jesus. Therefore, for the Honour and Glory of Christ, and for the long-suppressed Truth, and for the sake of this beloved and noble Philosophy, Magic, and Alchemy, as also for God's sake, I call upon persons of high and low degree to assist me with such writings. For the same they shall be humbly and gratefully rewarded when we (D.V.) shortly reach our goal in Philosophy and Medicine. For then shall they learn and appreciate the truth of that which we and others have long sought for.

"What though adverse omens be scanned by a reprobate world! Yet the goddess will fully triumph at last.

"Sacred Truth is always enshrouded in darkness."

Generous masters and friends, as regards the present little book, called by me " The New Golden and Olympic Pandora," I have wished to publish the same (faithfully and without guile, just as I have received it) for the benefit of disciples of the Spagyric Doctrine. It treats of the Philosopher's Stone, and has never appeared in print before. And, seeing that your Worships have for many years been special patrons of Alchemy and the Spagyric Art, possessing no little information and understanding in the same, I have wished to publish this book under your noble patronage, humbly begging you to accept thereof as from a well-known, yet poor disciple of the Theophrastian and Immortal Christian Philosophy, and to defend me and this philosophical book against all slanderers, mockers, and persecutors of these beloved Arts, and to assist in promoting and confirming the truth in every way. For which protection and favour, I will, by God's Grace and Blessing, faithfully testify my gratitude by word and deed.

Herewith commend I all and each of us to the Gracious Ward and Protection of God.

Done in our Scholarly Hermit's Cell, near Hagenau, on the day after the Festival of the Birth of Jesus Christ, our Trismegistus Spagyrus, into this world, December 26th, 1607.

Your Worships', etc., etc.,

Most Officious Servant,

BENEDICTUS FIGULUS,

Of Utenhofen, Fr. Poet; L. C. Theologian; Theosopher; Philosopher; Physician; Hermit, T. M.

THE BOOK OF THE REVELATION OF HERMES,

INTERPRETED BY

THEOPHRASTUS PARACELSUS,

CONCERNING

THE SUPREME SECRET OF THE WORLD.

HERMES, Plato, Aristotle, and the other philosophers, flourishing at different times, who have introduced the Arts, and more especially have explored the secrets of inferior Creation, all these have eagerly sought a means whereby man's body might be preserved from decay and become endued with immortality. To them it was answered that there is nothing which might deliver the mortal body from death; but that there is One Thing which may postpone decay, renew youth, and prolong short human life (as with the Patriarchs). For death was laid as a punishment upon our first parents, Adam and Eve, and will never depart from all their descendants. Therefore, the above philosophers, and many others, have sought this One Thing with great labour, and have found that that which preserves the human body from corruption, and prolongs life, conducts itself, with respect to other elements, as it were like the Heavens; from which they understood that the Heavens are a substance above the Four Elements. And just as the Heavens, with respect to the other elements, are held to be the fifth substance (for they are indestructible, stable, and suffer no foreign admixture), so also this One Thing (compared to the forces of our body) is an indestructible essence, drying up all the superfluities of our bodies, and has been philosophically called by the above-mentioned name. It is neither hot and dry like fire, nor cold and moist like water, nor warm and moist like air, nor dry and cold like earth. But it is a skilful, perfect equation of all the Elements, a right commingling of natural forces, a most particular union of spiritual virtues, an indissoluble uniting of body and soul. It is the purest and noblest substance of an indestructible body, which cannot be destroyed nor harmed by the Elements, and is produced by Art. With this Aristotle prepared an apple prolonging life by its scent, when he, fifteen days before his death, could neither eat nor drink on account of old age. This spiritual Essence, or One Thing, was revealed from above to Adam, and was greatly desired by the Holy Fathers, this also Hermes and Aristotle call the Truth without Lies, the most sure of all things certain, the Secret of all Secrets. It is the Last and the Highest Thing to be sought under the Heavens, a wondrous closing and finish of philosophical work, by which are discovered the dews of Heaven and the fastnesses of Earth. What the mouth of man cannot utter is all found in this spirit. As Morienus says: "He who has this has all things, and wants no other aid. For in it are all temporal happiness, bodily health, and earthly fortune. It is the spirit of the fifth substance, a Fount of all Joys (beneath the rays of the moon), the Supporter of of Heaven and Earth, the Mover of Sea and Wind, the Outpourer of Rain, upholding the strength of all things, an excellent spirit above Heavenly and other spirits, giving Health, Joy, Peace, Love; driving away Hatred and Sorrow, bringing in Joy, expelling all Evil, quickly healing all Diseases, destroying Poverty and Misery, leading to all good things, preventing all evil words and thoughts, giving man his heart's desire, bringing to the pious earthly honour and long life, but to the wicked who misuse it, Eternal Punishment."

This is the Spirit of Truth, which the world cannot comprehend without the interposition of the Holy Ghost, or without the instruction of those who know it. The same is of a mysterious nature, wondrous strength, boundless power. The Saints, from the beginning of the world, have desired to behold its face. By Avicenna this Spirit is named the Soul of the World. For, as the Soul moves all the limbs of the Body, so also does this Spirit move all bodies. And as the Soul is in all the limbs of the Body, so also is this Spirit in all elementary created things. It is sought by many and found by few. It is beheld from afar and found near; for it exists in every thing, in every place, and at all times. It has the powers of all creatures; its action is found in all elements, and the qualities of all things are therein, even in the highest perfection. By virtue of this essence did Adam and the Patriarchs preserve their health and live to an extreme age, some of them also flourishing in great riches.

When the philosophers had discovered it, with great diligence and labour, they straightway concealed it under a strange tongue, and in parables, lest the same should become known to the unworthy, and the pearls be cast before swine. For if everyone knew it, all work and industry would cease; man would desire nothing but this one thing, people would live wickedly, and the world be ruined, seeing that they would provoke God by reason of their avarice and superfluity. For eye hath not seen, nor ear heard, nor hath the heart of man understood what Heaven hath naturally incorporated with this Spirit. Therefore have I briefly enumerated some of the qualities of this Spirit, to the Honour of God, that the pious may reverently praise Him in His gifts (which gift of God shall afterwards come to them), and I will herewith shew what powers and virtues it possesses in each thing, also its outward appearance, that it may be more readily recognised.

In its first state, it appears as an impure earthly body, full of imperfections. It then has an earthly nature, healing all sickness and wounds in the bowels of man, producing good and consuming proud flesh, expelling all stench, and healing generally, inwardly and outwardly.

In its second nature, it appears as a watery body, somewhat more beautiful than before, because (although still having its corruptions) its Virtue is greater. It is much nearer the Truth, and more effective in works. In this form it cures cold and hot fevers, and is a specific against poisons, which it drives from heart and lungs, healing the same when injured or wounded, purifying the blood, and, taken three times a day, is of great comfort in all diseases.

But in its third nature it appears as an aërial body, of an oily nature, almost freed from all imperfections, in which form it does many wondrous works, producing beauty and strength of body, and (a small quantity being taken in the food) preventing melancholy and heating of the gall, increasing the quantity of the blood and seed, so that frequent bleeding becomes necessary. It expands the blood vessels, cures withered limbs, restores strength to the sight, in growing persons removes what is superfluous and makes good defects in the limbs.

In its fourth nature it appears in a fiery form (not quite freed from all inperfections, still somewhat watery and not dried enough), wherein it has many virtues, making the old young and reviving those at the point of death. For if to such an one there be given, in wine, a barleycorn's weight of this fire, so that it reach the stomach, it goes to his heart, renewing him at once, driving away all previous moisture and poison, and restoring the natural heat of the liver. Given in small doses to old people, it removes the diseases of age, giving the old young hearts and bodies. Hence it is called the Elixir of Life.

In its fifth and last nature, it appears in a glorified and illuminated form, without defects, shining like gold and silver, wherein it possesses all previous powers and virtues in a higher and more wondrous degree. Here its natural works are taken for miracles.

When applied to the roots of dead trees they revive, bringing forth leaves and fruit. A lamp, the oil of which is mingled with this spirit, continues to burn for ever without diminution. It converts crystals into the most precious stones of all colours, equal to those from the mines, and does many other incredible wonders which may not be revealed to the unworthy.

For it heals all dead and living bodies without other medicine. Here Christ is my witness that I lie not, for all heavenly influences are united and combined therein.

This essence also reveals all treasures in earth and sea, converts all metallic bodies into gold, and there is nothing like unto it under Heaven.

This spirit is the secret, hidden from the beginning, yet granted by God to a few holy men for the revealing of these riches to His Glory—dwelling in fiery form in the air, and leading earth with itself to Heaven, while from its body there flow whole rivers of living water.

This spirit flies through the midst of the Heavens like a morning mist, leads its burning fire into the water, and has its shining realm in the heavens.

And although these writings may be regarded as false by the reader, yet to the initiated they are true and possible, when the hidden sense is properly understood. For God is wonderful in his works, and his wisdom is without end.

This spirit in its fiery form is called a Sandaraca, in the aërial a Kybrick, in the watery an Azoth, in the earthly Alcohoph and Aliocosoph. Hence they are deceived by these names who, seeking without instruction, think to find this Spirit of Life in things foreign to our Art. For although this spirit which we seek, on account of its qualities, is called by these names, yet the same is not in these bodies and cannot be in them. For a refined spirit cannot appear except in a body suitable to its nature. And, by however many names it be called, let no one imagine there be different spirits, for, say what one will, there is but one spirit working everywhere and in all things.

That is the spirit which, when rising, illumines the Heavens, when setting incorporates the purity of Earth, and when brooding has embraced the Waters. This spirit is named Raphael, the Angel of God, the subtlest and purest, whom the others all obey as their King.

This spiritual substance is neither heavenly nor hellish, but an airy, pure, and hearty body, midway between the highest and lowest, without reason, but fruitful in works, and the most select and beautiful of all other heavenly things.

This work of God is far too deep for understanding, for it is the last, greatest, and highest secret of Nature. It is the Spirit of God, which in the Beginning filled the earth and brooded over the waters, which the world cannot grasp without the gracious interposition of the Holy Spirit and instruction from those who know it, which also the whole world desires for its virtue, and which cannot be prized enough. For it reaches to the planets, raises the clouds, drives away mists, gives its light to all things, turns everything into Sun and Moon, bestows all health and abundance of treasure, cleanses the leper, brightens the eyes, banishes sorrow, heals the sick, reveals all hidden treasures, and, generally, cures all diseases.

Through this spirit have the philosophers invented the Seven Liberal Arts, and thereby gained their riches. Through the same Moses made the golden vessels in the Ark, and King Solomon did many beautiful works to the honour of God. Therewith Moses built the Tabernacle, Noah the Ark, Solomon the Temple. By this Ezra restored the Law, and Miriam, Moses' sister, was hospitable; Abraham, Isaac, and Jacob, and other righteous men, have had lifelong abundance and riches; and all the saints possessing it have therewith praised God. Therefore is its acquisition very hard, more than that of gold and silver. For it is the best of all things, because, of all things mortal that man can desire in this world, nothing can compare with it, and in it alone is truth. Hence it is called the Stone and Spirit of Truth; in its works is no vanity, its praise cannot be sufficiently expressed. I am unable to speak enough of its virtues, because its good qualities and powers are beyond human thoughts, unutterable by the tongue of·man, and in it are found the properties of all things. Yea, there is nothing deeper in Nature.

O unfathomable abyss of God's Wisdom, which thus hath united and comprised in the virtue and power of this One Spirit the qualities of all existing bodies! O unspeakable honour and boundless joy granted to mortal man! For the destructible things of Nature are restored by virtue of the said Spirit.

O mystery of mysteries, most secret of all secret things, and healing and medicine of all things! Thou last discovery in earthly natures, last best gift to Patriarchs and Sages, greatly desired by the whole world! Oh, what a wondrous and laudable spirit is purity, in which stand all joy, riches, fruitfulness of life, and art of all arts, a power which to its initiates grants all material joys! O desirable knowledge, lovely above all things beneath the circle of the Moon, by which Nature is strengthened, and heart and limbs are renewed, blooming youth is preserved, old age driven away, weakness destroyed, beauty in its perfection preserved, and abundance ensured in all things pleasing to men! O thou spiritual substance, lovely above all things! O thou wondrous power, strengthening all the world! O thou invincible virtue, highest of all that is, although despised by the ignorant, yet held by the wise in great praise, honour and glory, that — proceeding from humours — wakest the dead, expellest diseases, restorest the voice of the dying!

O thou treasure of treasures, mystery of mysteries, called by Avicenna "an unspeakable substance," the purest and most perfect soul of the world, than which there is nothing more costly under Heaven, unfathomable in nature and power, wonderful in virtue and works, having no equal among creatures, possessing the virtues of all bodies under Heaven! For from it flow the water of life, the oil and honey of eternal healing, and thus hath it nourished them with honey and water from the rock. Therefore, saith Morienus: "He who hath it, the same also hath all things." Blessed art Thou, Lord God of our fathers, in that Thou hast given the prophets this knowledge and understanding, that they have hidden these things (lest they should be discovered by the blind, and those drowned in worldly godlessness) by which the wise and pious have praised Thee! For the discoverers of the mystery of this thing to the unworthy are breakers of the seal of Heavenly Revelation, thereby offending God's Majesty, and bringing upon themselves many misfortunes and the punishments of God.

Therefore, I beg all Christians, possessing this knowledge, to communicate the same to nobody, except it be to one living in Godliness, of well-proved virtue, and praising God, Who has given such a treasure to man. For many seek, but few find it. Hence the impure and those living in vice are unworthy of it. Therefore is this Art to be shewn to all God-fearing persons, because it cannot be bought with a price. I testify before God that I lie not, although it appear impossible to fools, that no one has hitherto explored Nature so deeply.

The Almighty be praised for having created this Art and for revealing it to God-fearing men. Amen.

And thus is fulfilled this precious and excellent work, called the revealing of the occult spirit, in which lie hidden the secrets and mysteries of the world.

But this spirit is one genius, and Divine, wonderful, and lordly power. For it embraces the whole world, and overcomes the Elements and the fifth Substance.

To our Trismegistus Spagyrus,
Jesus Christ,
Be praise and glory immortal.
Amen.

Concerning the True Medicine
of the
Most Distinguished Man,
Alexander von Suchten,
Doctor of Medicine and of Philosophy.

An Elegy to Charles of Salzburg.

THE Song begun was left unfinished, for he, who was to all as the Sun's light, perished.

The Knowledge of Medicine, by which Podilavius, Machaon, Apollo, and Hippocrates were famous, is not to be sought from Galenus, Avicenna, Mesnis, and other writers of this stamp, but from Magic; and he, who shall have rightly perceived the same, shall at length cure all diseases admitting of cure from death. But Magic has three Books:

Firstly, Theology; Secondly, Medicine; and Thirdly, Astronomy.

Whence the Magus knows and worships Trinity in Unity, and imparts the power he receives from God to suffering mortals. And those, be they Theologians, Astronomers, or Physicians, who shew not by their works what they profess with their mouths, are Caco-Magi and Pseudo-Prophets. By their fruits shall ye know them!

XVII. Positions by which it is clearly demonstrated what a Physician is, and what his Medicine, also by means of what remedies diseases are expelled from human bodies.

1. All diseases, whatever their nature, have their origin, or lie hidden in one of the principal members.

2. Diseases can only be expelled by the generation of good blood in the diseased member.

3. Good blood is generated by the nourishing of the sick member by means of digesting heat.

4. By sickness natural heat is impeded, whereby nourishment digests less.

5. Unless food be digested, blood is not generated.

6. Natural heat, by which everything is digested for sustaining and multiplication of individuals, is the heat of the Sun and Moon.

7. If the heat of the Sun and Moon existing in human bodies be impeded by any disease, whereby it does its office less effectually, it is to be comforted with the heat of Sun and Moon of the greater world, or with those things in which is the most potent virtue of Sun and Moon, applied by art.

8. The heat of the Sun and Moon of the greater world cannot comfort the heat of the Sun and Moon of the lesser world except it be conjoined with the same, *i.e.*, be converted into a simple spirit, like the spirit of our life, which is done by dissolving it in nutriment.

9. Nutriment, or that matter remaining in the stomach after the separation of superfluities, is a crude and undigested thing, convertible by natural heat into the substance of our bodies.

10. The heat of the Sun and Moon is extracted, by a wonderful and occult art, from those things through which matter is most simply generated by the great and good God, from the Spirit of the World, for the restoration and conservation of human nature. The same is entirely unknown to Galenus, Avicenna, and all the other physicians of our time, who seek medicines in apothecaries' shops.

11. The spirit of the World and the spirit of our bodies are one and the same spirit. Therefore the heat of Sun and Moon, generated from the food itself of this spirit, is a thing more decocted and digested, and consequently more perfect, and is called, by Plato Nature of the World, and by Pythagorean Philosophers Primal Mind, Divine Intellect, Image of Divine Intelligence, Visible Son of God; Orpheus, a most ancient theologian, calls it Jupiter; Dionysius, a disciple of St. Paul, names it a Visible Image of God.

12. For that heat is a most perfect

spiritual entity, the greatest among all God's creatures, and the nutriment in the stomach is the imperfect, corporeal matter, undergoing transmutation.

13. Therefore we have here a task which, in some measure, has reference to both, viz.: Solar and Spiritual Heat, and Material Nutriment, which medium is also called by philosophers the Fifth Essence.

14. The heat of Sun and Moon, Fifth Essence, and Nutriment, when thus mixed in our bodies, produces the purest blood in which is heavenly virtue, freeing us from all disease, which nothing else in the whole world can do. For there are in this compound the virtues of all celestial and terrestrial bodies, so that the whole world is present in one drop of this same medicine.

15. The Fifth Essence alone, by the aid of the physician, brings about durable health, which physician, however, is not Galena, nor Avicenna, nor Rhasis, nor Mesne, nor Serapio, but the same heat of Sun and Moon, the

treasure of the wise, and inestimable glory of the whole world.

16. The Fifth Essence is neither known by apothecaries nor sold in their shops. Therefore, apothecaries prepare not medicines, but rather poisons, with which they corrupt the complexion of the human body.

17. The heat of Sun and Moon is not to be met with in the Schools of Bologna, Padua, Ferraria, Paris, Louvain, or Wittenberg. Therefore, Doctors of Medicine graduating there are not physicians, but impostors and cheats, who, entering the temple of Apollo, not by the door but through the roof, occupy his seat, even as did the Scribes and Pharisees the seat of Moses.

Therefore, not without cause do those whose intellect is obscured by the precepts and traditions of fools, and are hence unwilling to follow the wise, knowing the secrets of Nature, and curing so-called incurable maladies by natural means, accuse them of having a devil. For if they owned that these cures had been effected by means of that Medical Science, the very threshold of which they have never crossed, then doubtless all men would know them to be no physicians, but impostors and shedders of human blood.

Christ, Theologian, Astronomer, Physician.

To Christ alone be Glory. Amen.

MAN, THE BEST AND MOST PERFECT OF GOD'S CREATURES.

A More Complete Exposition of this Medical Foundation for the Less Experienced Student.

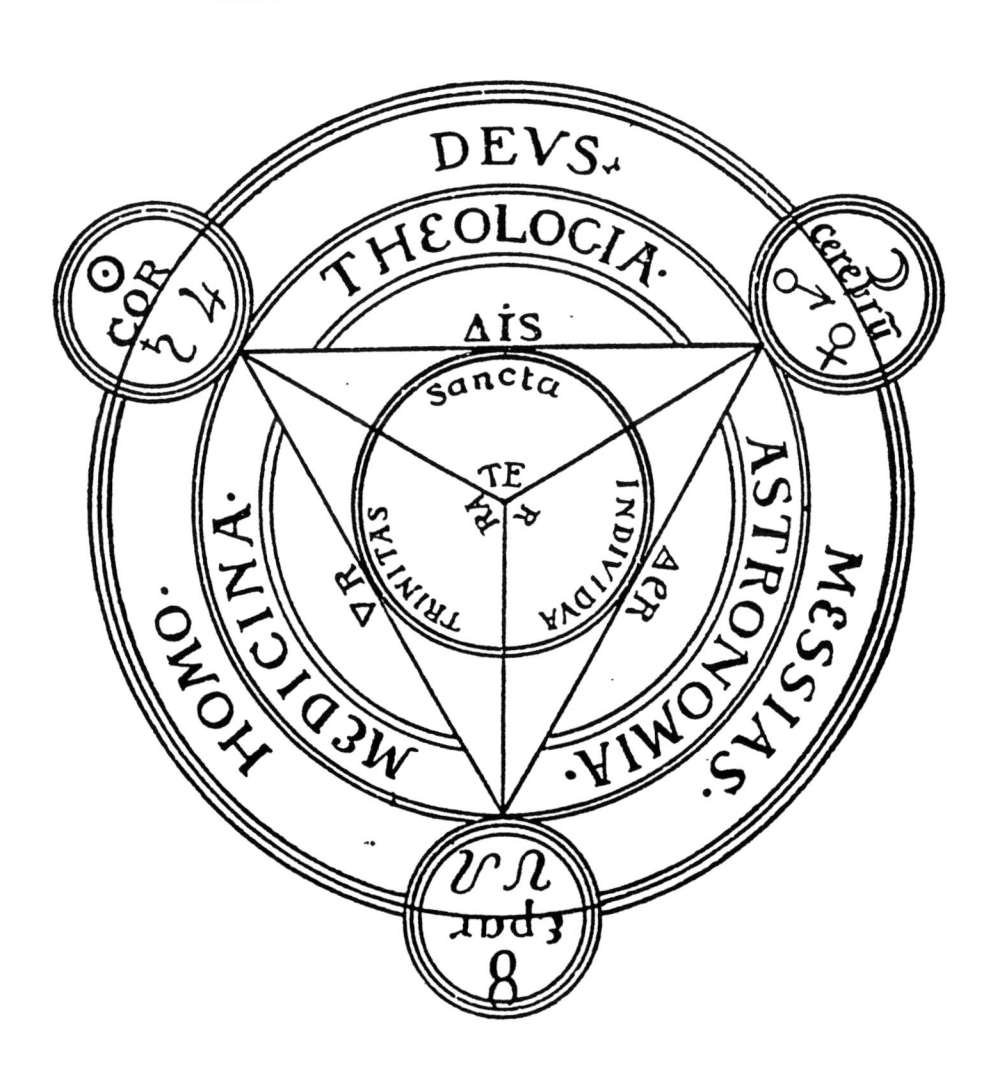

ARISTOTLE says that every form of every nature, animal, vegetable, and mineral, is produced by the power of matter, intrinsically, except the Human Soul, which, being of a different and higher nature than matter, is given, extrinsically, by the Prime Motor, God Himself. It is this thing concerning which, all theologians and physicians disputing, nevertheless mostly conclude the Soul of Man to be not produced from a germ, but, as it were, to be inspired and poured into the fœtus in its mother's womb, by God the Author of all life.

But, since two different things cannot be mixed or joined into one, and the Soul being a certain Divine light and substance, emanating immortal from Divine springs, so produced, incorporeally, that it is dependent on the virtue of the Agent, not on the bosom of matter, the same is a *primum mobile*, and, as they say, spontaneous and self-moving: And, on the other hand, the

Body is wholly earthly matter, having its origin in gross, rank, elementary matter, mortal of itself, unfit for motion, and therefore far inferior to the Soul; wherefore it can never be united to the Soul, so different from itself, except through a third, a medium participating in the nature of each, a quasi-body and quasi-soul, by which the Soul may be added and joined to the Body.

But such medium they suppose to be the Spirit or Soul of the World, *i.e.*, what we call Fifth Essence, because it consists not of the four elements, but is a certain fifth one, above and beside them. Such Spirit necessarily requires, as it were, a binding-chain, whereby Celestial Souls may bestow on grosser bodies strength and wondrous gifts; as also God and Man cannot be united except through a Medium, our Saviour Christ, participating in the two natures, Celestial and Terrestrial, Divine and Human. But this spirit is of the same form in the greater world as in the lesser, *i.e.*, the human body, our spirit, which arises from the former, and is with it one and the same spirit.

For, as the forces of our soul are through the natural spirit applied to the members, so is the virtue of the World's soul diffused through all things by the same spirit, or fifth essence. For the life and forces of all inferior species, which philosophers are wont to call souls or lives, are distributed by that ethereal or celestial spirit throughout all the elements, as it were, by the members, into the body of the Universal World, first by God Himself, then by intelligent beings, then by the stars, and lastly by the Sun, as it were the Heart of Heaven. And, again, this Spirit being taken away, bodies return to that whence they came; and thus the Human Soul, according to the Platonic School, proceeding from Highest Heaven, from God Himself, is, by proper media, joined to our viler body. In that first descent, also, the soul is enfolded in the ethereal and ardent corpuscle which they call the ethereal vehicle of the Soul, while we name it the Spirit of the World and Fifth Essence. Through this medium, by command of God, Who is the Centre of the greater world, the Soul descends and is poured into the heart, which is the centre of the lesser world (*i.e.*, the human body), and from thence is diffused through all the parts and members of its body, when, joining its vehicle (or chariot) to natural heat, through the spiritual heat born in the heart, the Soul is immersed in the blood, and by it equally diffused in the members. Thus it is patent how the Immortal Soul is enclosed in this viler body, viz., by means of the ethereal vehicle. But when the bonds between the Celestial Soul and natural vital spirit are loosened by disease, then the Soul, withdrawing from the members, flows back to the heart, the first receptacle of Soul and Life. From the heart, the Soul, leaving the vital natural spirit, flies away with its vehicle into the Heavens, when, being followed by guardian genii and demons, they lead it before the Judge.

Then, according to the Sentence, God joyfully conducts the good souls to glory, but a raging demon snatches away the bad to punishment. And the Body returns to the earth whence it came. Thus man dies. Hence it is plain that the daily preserving of the Soul in the body—that is, our life—and the avoiding of diseases, and that greatest dissolution of Soul and Body, called death, depend on the vehicle of the Soul, viz., the Celestial and our natural Spirit, and so the same has been by various authors called by different names. Some term it Spirit or Soul of the World, others Celestial Fire, others again Vital Spirit, Natural Heat, by which nothing else is denoted than that oft mentioned Spirit of things celestial and inferior, the *gluten* of Body and Soul. On examining the thing more fully, this is simply the heat and humour of Sun and Moon, for we know the administration of the Heavens and all bodies under the Heavens to be appointed to the Sun and Moon; the Sun is the Lord of all virtues of the elements; the Moon, by virtue of the Sun. the mistress of generation, of increase and decrease. Hence Albumansar says that life is poured into all things through the Moon and Sun; and therefore they are called by Orpheus the vivifying eyes of Heaven. Whence also the saying— the Sun and man generate man; for the Sun sits as a King among the planets, in magnitude, beauty, and light excelling all, illuminating all, dispensing virtue to them as well as to inferior things, and abundantly bestowing light and life, not only in Heaven and the Air, but also in the earth and profoundest depths of the Abyss. Whatever good we possess is from the Sun whence Heraclitus deservedly calls it the Fount of Heavenly Light, and many of the Platonic School have located the World's Soul principally therein, which Soul, filling the Sun's whole globe, pours its rays (or spirit) everywhere, throughout all things, distributing Life, Sense, and Motion to the Universe itself. And as in animate beings the heart rules the whole body, so does the Sun rule and govern Heaven and Earth and all that in them is. But the Moon, the Earth's nearest neighbour, by the velocity of its monthly course, is joined to the Sun and other planets, and receiving their rays and influences as in an espousal, and, as it were, bringing forth, communicates to and sheds upon its near neighbour, the earth, all life and motion.

From these two founts arises that mundane, natural, and vital spirit, permeating all entities, giving to all things life and consistence, binding, moving, and filling all things, Immense Renewer in Nature's charge, through whom, as a mediator, every hidden property, every virtue, all life, are propagated in inferior bodies, in herbs, in metals, in stones, in things animate, so that, in the whole world, there is nothing wanting in a spark of this spirit. For it is in all things, penetrating through all; it is diffused in stones (being struck from the same by steel); it is in the water (which smokes in ditches); and in the earth (which heats springs and wells). It is in the depths of the sea (becoming warm when agitated by the wind), and in the air (which we often perceive to grow hot); also all animals and all things living are nourished by heat, and all sentient beings do live by reason of their latent heat. Whence Virgil says this inward principle nourishes heaven and earth, the sunlit plains, the glowing orb of the Moon, and the Tithonian Stars. The same is elsewhere called: That Vigour and Celestial Origin. Therefore this spirit, when whole and undiminished in our bodies, and not impeded by things extraneous, is our natural heat, by which everything is digested for the sustenance and multiplying of individuals.

For it digests man's food, generating good blood in all his members. Now, with pure blood there is a strong, pure, and healthy vital spirit of the heart, and thus the whole body is healthy. But if, by some impediment, it does its office less fully, there arises bad decoction of nutriment, whence generation of impure blood. By this the heart's vital spirit is weakened, whence arises old age and, at length, full extinction, consumption, and dissipation of that spirit, which is natural death. Therefore, to avoid this, the said spirit and natural heat, thus diminished, or impeded, must be increased and comforted that it may better and more strongly perform its functions. But as agents act not with inferiors but with equals, so also must this comforting take place through the spirit's equal, viz., through the celestial heat of Sun and Moon and other planets, or with those things in which the virtue of Sun and Moon are most potent, abundant, and least bound up with matter. For these things act more quickly and effectually; they generate their like more promptly, and from them is more easily obtained that Spirit or Celestial Fire whose properties are heat, not consuming like the elementary, but fructifying all things; and light, bestowing life on all things. But the properties of elementary and inferior fire are burning, consuming all things, and filling them with barrenness and darkness. Therefore is the same excluded, as also all other inferior and elementary subjects. For all these things of natural composition, and not freed from grosser matter, are subject to corruption and transmutation. Now, medicines ought, all the more, to be durable and free from corruption, since they are to cure the human body from corruption; otherwise they would do more harm than good. I add that it would be vain to preserve the corruptible body by a putrid and corruptible thing, or to attempt to heal an infirm nature with a thing infirm, or yet to fashion a thing by deformity. For the corruptible, infirm, and weak added to its like increases the corruptibility and does not diminish it. Thus we see many, and even most, of the physicians of our time in vain attempt to heal, and secure immunity from disease, by means of the crass and corporeal compositions of their medicaments. But this speculation goes farther. For diseases which are spiritual, not corporeal, also demand spiritual medicines. Therefore, to those wishing to preserve that vital spirit in the young (which is the humid and warm radical), to restore the lost powers in old men and to bring them back, as it were, to youth, and to educe to their highest perfection the powers of man's life, I would say that such will do well to seek, not the Elemental, but that Celestial heat of Sun and Moon, dwelling in a more incorruptible substance, under the Moon's intermittent orb, and to make this similar to our heat or spirit; so that, prepared as medicine and sweetest food, when taken into the mouth it may immediately penetrate the human frame, greatly holding to itself every fleshly thing, increasing, restoring, and nourishing the incorrupt virtue and spirit of life, digesting the crude and undigested, removing the superfluous, making natural water abound, and augmenting, comforting, and inflaming natural heat or fire.

The above will be the duty of the true physician and sane philosopher. For thus will he be able to preserve our body from corruption, to retard old age, retain florid youth in full vigour, and, if it be possible, to perpetuate it, at least to preserve it from death and destruction. But we here speak of natural death philosophically, which is only a natural consumption of moisture and heat, as is demonstrated by a lighted lamp; not theologically, of that fatal death and last end of Nature destined by God for each one, by which we are compelled not only to pay our debt, but also, by reason of our sins, to suffer punishment. For we know that, for his sins, man must once die, Job saying: "Seeing his days are determined, the number of his months are with Thee; Thou hast appointed his bounds that he cannot pass,"—which text plainly sets forth that these bounds, once constituted by God, cannot be passed by human aid or skill; for which cause also Adam was driven forth from the Paradise of Joy, lest, after the Fall, he should become equally as immortal as before by eating of the Tree of Life. Neither is it credible that, outside Paradise, God should have given Adam anything whereby he and his descendants might live for ever, when by the very expulsion He forthwith deprived Adam of access to the Tree of Life. Therefore no aid can be found, still less invented, beyond those last bounds set us by God. On the other hand, there is a remedy against many infirmities, and against the weakening of radical moisture and innate heat.

For Adam, created by God full of understanding and perfect knowledge of natural things, doubtless knew those which were capable of prolonging human life and securing immunity from disease. Doubtless he also taught the same to some of his descendants, and they again to others. Hence many of the Fathers lived to the age of 700, 800, and more years; but some did not live so long, this secret not being revealed to all.

Therefore it is conceded that (on this side of that limit of death) there may be found something to restore our sick body. For just as man, through disease and other causes, often fails to reach to the appointed limit of life, so, on the other hand, by removing these impediments, he may prolong life to the very utmost limit set him.

But some may affirm that such a medicine cannot be found in the whole sphere of this nether world, because all things created, being either elements or composed of and congenital with them, are therefore corruptible, and hence that this medicine and incorruptible root of life can nowhere be found. Those speaking thus learnedly, without having ever entered the Sanctuary of Nature, fail to consider there is in the elements something beside corruptible qualities. For the elements and their compounds, in addition to crass matter, are composed of a subtle substance, or intrinsic radical humidity, diffused through the elemental parts, simple and wholly incorruptible, long preserving the things themselves in vigour, and called the Spirit of the World, proceeding from the Soul of the World, the one certain life, filling and fathoming all things, gathering together and connecting all things, so that from the three genera of creatures, Intellectual, Celestial, and Corruptible, there is formed the One Machine of the whole world.

This Spirit by its virtue fecundates all subjects natural and artificial, pouring into them those hidden properties which we have been wont to call the Fifth Essence. We do not say that Medicine is quite as incorruptible as Heaven (or it could not in the stomach be converted into nutriment), but, being generated from matter above all others and incorruptible with respect to them, and simply formed by the separation therefrom of all corruptible elements, it could be kept, if necessary, 10,000 years.

For this cause skilful physicians advise us to use less incorruptible (indigestible?) food. This thing has the same bearing with respect to the four qualities of our body as Heaven has with respect to the four elements. For Heaven is called by philosophers the Fifth Essence with respect to the four elements, because Heaven is in itself incorruptible, immutable, not receiving foreign impressions, unless acting on the elements by God's command.

Thus the thing we seek is, in relation to the four qualities of our body, a Fifth Essence, incorruptible in itself, made by art. It is not hot and dry like fire, for it cools hot things, diminishing and expelling fevers; nor does it cool humid things like water, for it burns, which is repugnant to the element water. Nor, again, does it moisten hot things, like air, for it corrupts not like air, which is easily decomposed, as we see in the generation of spiders and flies; nor is it cold and dry like the earth, for it sharpens and warms. But it supplies to each its contrary quality, like unto the incorruptible Heaven, which, according to necessity, furnishes the hot, cold, moist, or dry quality, and just as Supreme Heaven does not by itself alone preserve the world, but through the virtue of the Sun, Moon, and other Stars, so also does this our Heaven, or Fifth Essence, wish and deserve to be adorned by a splendid, wondrous, and occult Sun, from which it has incorruptibility, virtue, and heat.

But this is the root of life, *i.e.*, the Fifth Essence, created by the Almighty for the preservation of the four qualities of the human body, even as Heaven is for the preservation of the Universe. Therefore in this Fifth Essence and Spiritual Medicine, which is of Nature and the Heat of Heaven, and not of a mortal or corrupt quality, is indeed possible the Fount of Medicine, the preservation of life, the restoration of health, and in this may the cherished desire for the renewal of lost youth and serene health be found. For, briefly, in the whole world there is no better medicine than this. Even as in every genus there is something holding the first rank in that genus, so also this Medicine, being prepared from the most efficacious and incorruptible matter under Heaven, viz., from the Soul and Spirit of the World, containing within itself the virtues of all things celestial and terrestrial, will hold the first rank among medicines, and man, by using the same, together with other food, in moderation, may attain to the age of the Patriarchs. For of this composition, combining as it does the virtues of all things, there may truly be said that in one drop the whole world is present. It is this most famous medicine which philosophers have been wont to call their Stone, or Powder. This is its fount and fundament, and the Medicine whereby Æsculapius raised the dead. This is the herb by which Medea restored Jason to life. This is the secret substance brought from Colchis by the Argonauts under Jason with so much journeying and pains, and hence called the Golden Fleece; partly because this Science excels in virtue all others, as the Sun does the stars and gold the other metals; and partly because that Fleece was a Book written with golden letters (according to the testimony of Suidas, Historiographer of the Chemical and Medical Arts), and containing a full account of the preparation of the Medicine. For in that Book is the first material for the creation, restoration, and preservation of our most true Medicine.

Chemistry can be easily understood by the intelligent, and chemistry, *i.e.*, altering metals, may properly be included in the teaching of the theory of the True Medicine aforesaid, both flowing from the same fount, namely, the World's Soul, which, being, as it were, the only life of things, and the author of generation, will contain within itself the seeds of all inferior natures.

In harmonious order it rules, vivifies, and fecundates. But, for younger disciples, it has pleased us to describe somewhat more fully the principles of chemistry, which each one may easily prove for himself. For, when he has considered the matter, he will perceive that God would be compelled, perpetually and each moment, to create new creatures, lest the species of all things in that beautiful house, the universal world, should perish entirely, had He not, when breathing the breath of life into man and all other beings, at the same time given them the command: "Increase and multiply in the earth." By which breath and command He imparted unto them not only natural life, or a living soul, but also the power, which may be called the generative spirit, whereby every genus may preserve and perpetuate its race eternally. For everything which may generate is necessarily alive, as, on the other hand, that having life, unless prevented, will generate. Therefore, at the Creation the generative spirit began the order of continuous production which shall only cease with the world.

Hence God commanded Noah to build so great an Ark that it might receive and save from destruction some of each species and both sexes, which, after the Deluge, should again propagate their kind.

And anyone attentively observing the universal world will doubtless perceive this perpetual order of generation everywhere, not only in these crass, inferior, elementated bodies, but also in the simple celestial bodies and in the elements themselves. Elements generate their own kind, as we are taught by the infallible rule of daily experience. A fire converts the matter it consumes into its own nature, viz , fire, thereby augmenting itself. Air does likewise, easily corrupting things and dissolving them into air like itself. Earth, foul and dissolved, becomes water; the latter, through heat made gross and dense, becomes earth; but, evaporated by heat, is changed into air, and this again, by overheating, into fire. Fire, when extinguished, returns to air, cooled air becomes water, and that again, by coagulation, earth. But the natural order of generation is more plainly perceived among inferior and composite bodies, which philosophers have divided into the three orders: Animals, Vegetables, Minerals. For these have their own seed, implanted by Nature herself, by which they manifestly and visibly produce similar fœtuses, thus augmenting their kind by propagation. From horse, man, bull, are respectively generated horse, man, and bull. Likewise all vegetables, herbs, trees, shrubs, cast their own seeds on to the ground, which, in course of time, produce species similar to themselves. Indeed, the minerals and metals lying hid in the very centre of the earth have also undergone the same changes, although their seed and generations are not visibly shewn, as in the preceding orders—for, by reason of the great mass of the earth concealing the hidden, contained seed, the same is by many believed neither to grow nor to generate.

But the attentive observer of Nature, its origin, increase, and incrementation, will certainly not dispute its possession of vital spirit and generative power, by which it not only originates and has nutriment, life, and consistence, but also must be admitted to possess the power of generating its kind. For everything increasing, originating, growing, and receiving nourishment has vegetative life, hence propagating power. And the reason of the generation of minerals not being so patent to the eye as that of vegetables and animals, is the earth's great and abundant fecundity, its vast mass, by which that spirit is restrained and impeded as in a prison and chains, by which it can less perform its functions and generate its kind. The same when freed by art from its terrestrial house and sepulchre, doubtless, like others, sharers of generative virtue, will be able to bring forth fruit by its seed, and thus metal will produce metal and gold generate gold.

From this it is manifest that the

generation of metals, and especially of gold, is not only permitted by God, and possible to Nature, but also to human art. Consequently the Art of Chemistry is not fictitious, not detestable, not base, as to-day it is falsely called by many, but true, admirable, holy, and well proven. For by natural means seeding out the invisible, impalpable, generative spirit, elsewhere called the Seed of Metals, it so treats the same that it bears fruit similar to itself, etc. Therefore, many philosophers, moved by this argument, have sought that golden seed in gold itself; and, having found what they wished, have cut out, or extracted, the same from a mass of gold, as it were, from the stones placed by Nature about it, which, being thus separated, and afterwards applied by them to anything of a like nature—*i.e.*, any metal—has immediately changed the same into gold and silver. Hence they have proved by experiment that gold can generate its like, but have thereby gained no lucre or emolument. For this spirit, or seed, of gold, when mixed with any of the other metals, can convert into gold only a quantity equal to the gold whence the seed was extracted, and not more. Hence the process was a tedious and most difficult one, requiring much time and a large outlay. That, therefore, this generation and manufacture of gold might be carried on more easily and abundantly, with less expense and yet with more profit and utility, the Ancient Sages were compelled to relinquish common gold, and, with the spirit of which we in this place treat, viz. the generating spirit of all creatures, were forced to seek a method of making gold elsewhere; in respect of which they spared neither labour, nor time, nor expense, and at length arrived at one thing in which all their wishes were fulfilled, for they obtained a nature, or body, or certain compound, in which the metallic, gold-producing spirit was unlimited and unstraitened, not limited in quantity proportionate to the matter, but so intense, exuberant, possessing more of form (essence) than of matter, that, by artificial fire, it may be reduced to its greatest purity, and may be so treated, diffused, extended, and multiplied that, after completion, it is a thousand thousand times stronger than bodies naturally perfect, *i.e.*, gold and silver.— For the more form a thing has, the more entity, virtue, and operation it has. Those things in which the idea (which is the form) is least merged into the body, or matter, have the most potent virtues, because being the most formal (spiritual), they can with very little matter effect very much. This matter thus formed and taken possession of by all sons of this science, lest it should become known to the unworthy, and equally that it might be known by the worthy, we read of as described by the sages in divers enigmatical ways only to be understood by the initiated. The following are some of the principal circumlocutions designed indirectly to make known this great secret: What is the strongest creature in the whole world, the most conservative, most penetrative, most volatile, the most unalterable and fixed in fire? The thing that fire has not touched is accessible and known to all men, of much superfluity, to be found everywhere, and by all. It is a part of man, begets and is begotten in man, is heavy in weight, soft (or at least not hard) to the touch, not rough, sweet to the taste but of a sharp nature, sweet to the smell but at the same time having a fetid and sepulchral odour, pleasant to sight and hearing, yet of obtuse sound, not the less fire for being almost wholly earth, nor yet simply water, neither very acute nor obtuse but mediocre in quality, revealed by reflection, various in colour, white, black, and last red, most easily fusible, and also of metallic fusion, without much sound, in action animal vegetable, and mineral. It is a thing which the earth produces and which descends from Heaven, both active and passive, masculine and feminine, consisting of Soul, Spirit, and Body.

It is the one subject of everything wonderful in Heaven and Earth, without which neither Alchemy, Medicine, nor Natural Magic can exhibit their complete aim. It is also the first and last, greatest of all creatures, by most commonly called red, or Adamic, Earth. From these and similar attributes, or circumstances, and in no other way, may this matter be known and prepared by a proper, natural method, at length excelling in that naturally desired by all, and pursued by all with great eagerness, viz., daily and healthy life, without all infirmity, until natural death. And it will further afford gold, silver, pearls, gems, and such precious things, as well as all that is necessary to the honest sustenance of life, abundantly and affluently. Thus the object of Chemistry is identical with that of Medicine, the same Spirit, same Heat, same Quintessence, the same Soul, Medium of Nature, which permits one thing to be converted into another; finally there are the same uses, rewards, and emoluments for the disciples of either Science who shall have known how to separate this Quintessence from its defilements and impurities, and to reduce it to pure simplicity. For he who shall have been able, from its impure and manifold elements, to convert it to purity and simplicity, discerning the nature, virtue, and power of these elements in their number, degrees, and order, without division of substance, the same is truly a Physician, natural Magus, and consummate Philosopher. For by the same heat of Sun and Moon, the same Spirit of the World, by which human bodies are healed from infirmities and accidents, he can restore imperfect or impure metals to True Health—which is Conversion into Gold—and thus he will have thoroughly discovered the whole virtue of Nature's occult operations, and will easily obtain a perfect knowledge and grasp of all natural and celestial secrets. On the other hand—if ignorant of all these things—he can attain to no knowledge of such wonderful agencies.

Hence it is plain that this art, and most secret of all Nature's secrets, is in vain attempted and sought by those who daily join themselves to princes and magnates, and immediately attempt Hermes Stone, the Sacred Stone, Philosophers' Mercury, all kinds of furnaces and burnings, strong waters, King of Antimony, perpetual fire, and many more inept things of that sort, and, with this gullible art in their mouths, promise whole mountains of gold; knowing, nevertheless, not a single word of Latin, and still less having tasted a single drop from Nature's hidden Founts. For unless one be instructed in the discipline of the great arts, he can become but little proficient therein. Wherefore the above has been collected from Natural, Mathematical, and Supernatural Precepts, etc.

Here follows the Practice—which, however, is wanting owing to the sudden death of the Excellent Author, A. V. S.

A DIALOGUE,

BY ALEXANDER VON SUCHTEN,

Doctor of Chemistry and Famous Philosopher,

INTRODUCING TWO INTERLOCUTORY PERSONAGES, VIZ., ALEXANDER AND BERNHARDUS.

ALEXANDER: That is the cause of my departure. I therefore beg you to give me the good counsel you have already been asked for by me.

Bernhardus: Why do you, an old Physician and Chemist, allow yourself to be misled by the popular cry? Know you not the way of the world, that he who praises not himself has no consideration? The popular cry should not have moved you to leave wife and child at home, wandering about and seeking in other lands what you might perhaps have found sooner and better at home. For old acquaintance sake, I will not refuse you the desired counsel. For, as you say, we were good friends in Italy, at Padua, Ferraria, Bologna, and Rome, when seeking there what we did not find. But, before I speak further with you, tell me what good have you experienced and learnt at Basel, Cologne, in Switzerland, on the Rhine, in Silesia, in the Marches (Brandenburg), and in Denmark, where you were with the Paracelsian doctors?

Alexander: As I came to them, so I left them; what they told me I had already read in Paracelsus, where he speaks of Flowers of Antimony, of Matter of Pearls, of Juice of Coral, of the virtues of Hellebore, of Potable Gold, and of the Quintessence. But I had thought to hear from these learned persons what Paracelsus means by those names and terms. For I had long remarked that his Vitriol and Tartar were not sulphuric acid and common tartar; and so on with the other names. But I saw the good gentlemen still read it literally. Hence I did not learn from them the mysteries hidden by Paracelsus under the said names. Each one has his preparations, highly praised by himself; but I ask not for preparations, knowing that in the things prepared by them there are not the secrets sought by us. I have spent much time and labour over the substances they occupy themselves with, which they, as Chemists of the New School, hold in great honour. But I think nothing of all that, as they also will find out in time. Hence you can easily guess what I have learnt from them.

Bernhardus: But I hear they do much with their Chemical Medicines?

Alexander: Yes, as luck will have it, sometimes much, sometimes little; as also happens with us Galenian doctors. Paracelsus writes that Medicine is a certain art, which a physician must be as fully master of as a tanner of his trade. He says not it is easier to learn than the tanner's trade. But such perfection have I found in none, and they all speak of different things and long labour. What shall I, then, think of these professors? I know you have earnestly occupied yourself with the secrets of medicine for the last 27 years, and I pray that you do not refuse your old true comrade what you, in that long period, have learnt concerning these hidden matters.

Bernhardus: Vitriol, Tartar, Coral, Pearls, Jewels, are not that upon which the Medicine of Paracelsus is built. For the first philosophers and inventors of medicine have spoken concerning weighty things in parables and other figures of speech. Thus also Paracelsus, who, in his teaching, has invented some names, having received others from the Ancients — excepting some in which Medicinal Virtues, but not perfections, are found. Marvel not that Paracelsian doctors take the similitude for truth.

Alexander: But I have left home to discover the same, yet have found no one to teach me. I well know there is something in Vitriol, also in Tartar, Antimony, Mercury, but find not in them what Paracelsus ascribes to them.

Bernhardus: Perhaps you know not the proper preparation of these substances.

Alexander: Bother the preparation! I see others do as little with their preparations as I with mine; therefore, there must be another reason for it.

Bernhardus: Have you read the chapter in Paracelsus concerning Dropsy? Therein you find the simples which may help to cure your brother of this complaint.

Alexander: Certainly, I have read it more than once, but what simples are there in it other than Mercurium Columbinum, Crocus, Sulphur, the Element of Fire, and Diaphoretic Gold? I would not put Mercury calcinated, precipitated, sublimated, etc., into my brother's mouth, neither would I Sulphur; and when I apply Columbinum, or Gallinaceum, and other poultices, according to our custom, they are of no avail. What Element of Fire is I know not. I do know that

Diaphoretic Gold, as Alchemists make it, with Mercury, acids, oil of salt, and with urine, is a poison—and that the Diaphoretic Gold of Paracelsus must be something else. Are Crocus and Sal Martis burnt iron, which is used by the doctor for restoring health?

Bernhardus: I plainly perceive that since you have taken a wife, are laden with domestic cares, and are practising according to the Galenian method to keep a family, you have ceased to reflect on these matters.

Alexander: I must make shift with Galenian Medicine until I can get a better master. Nevertheless, I always am working and seeking the arcana, but I have hitherto had little success; why, I know not, for I am not wanting in diligence.

Bernhardus: I will tell you. God is a Searcher of all minds, and Medicine is in His hand: He grants it according to our heart. When we were at Padua I know you took the opinions of Galenus for Gospel, that you graduated in the same, and that you then went with some other doctors to Friaul, there to try the new medicine. But what happened to you and your comrades? You thought you had collected from your professors the golden fleece of medicine,—no disease could resist you. Then you found that your fleece was nothing but asses' figs, and the peasants who ate the same died, or were crippled and lamed. Do you remember what a quarrel you thereupon had with your preceptors? But what answer did you get? That you were only a young doctor; that Practice was not so easily learned; that you must exercise yourself therein, and go on killing people, and at last you would become a clever doctor. That is also the experience of others who get their medicine from the universities. Hence it is a Gift of God, and comes not from Padua, Paris, or Wittenberg. He Himself has created and compounded medicine, not Galenus not Avicenna, not Paracelsus, but He alone, and from Him we must learn the Truth—not from this or that author. Each one has written according to the measure of Truth he has found. We may, therefore, take them for guides, but not for the way itself, as we did when spending our youth so uselessly at the High Schools. Since Galenus knew and described medicine, and his professors made a physician of thee, tell me, when thou seekest information from others, what does Paracelsus concern thee?

Alexander: Everyone knows that Paracelsus was a learned man who has written many clever things, but he invented not Medicine himself, having received it from Hippocrates and others. Therefore, God has bestowed upon him great understanding, whereby he has brought Medicine into a right order and one method, through which it has acquired a reputation not possessed by it before. Hence Galenus is so highly considered by the learned, and alone taught in the Schools. The reason for my having got into the Medicine of Paracelsus is this: I have long been a

Chemist, seeking that which others seek, and yet I cannot attain it, but find in Paracelsus that, by Alchemistic preparation, medicine should be made to act. I have also in High Germany heard of incredible cures effected by Paracelsus—as his Epitaph also testifies—and, therefore wished to make use of my chemical studies in preparing medicaments, thinking to discover the secrets of medicine if I might not make gold and silver. For I cannot deny that, since we have mighty principles and authors of our medicine, and yet can do so little in dangerous sickness, we must be, for some cause, deficient in medicine.

Bernhardus: Yes, truly, a great deficiency. You write and chatter much, and when at the patient's bedside, you cannot drive away a fever. You purge, anoint, and poultice in vain, putting him off with fine words and dieting, until Nature herself overcomes the disease; then you have excellently shewn your skill. But if he dies, killed by your quackery, the disease was incurable.

What shall I say of other maladies more serious than fevers? As you understand and treat the one, so you do the others. Tell me, on your conscience, can you, with your Galenian method, drive away a fever?

Alexander: I cannot do so with certainty. A doctor is but the minister of Nature, not her master.

Bernhardus: We know well that Nature herself is our medicine, and that she helps the sick person when the impediments are removed. With respect to these impediments we must assist Nature, but I have never seen one who could cure a fever, without fail, in a certain fixed time.

Alexander: I have known one, but cannot sufficiently wonder at the medicine.

Bernhardus: What think you is the cause that you Galenians cannot do so?

Alexander: That our theory has a false foundation I cannot assert, but must confess that the result does not correspond with the principles.

Bernhardus: Were the principles good, the result also could not fail to be so. But your principles were invented by phantastic, unlearned scatterbrains, who knew not Nature.

Alexander: You must not thus despise the famous and praiseworthy doctors; they are, after all, very learned men.

Bernhardus: I despise no one, but it is my duty to rescue the Truth. As the Greeks say: I am a friend of Socrates and Plato, but still more so of Truth. If Nature have not taught their principles, they are learned but with their own sort.

Alexander: Not only with their own sort, but at the Courts of Emperors, Kings, and Princes, and with many honest men.

Bernhardus: Your citing mighty Potentates only shews they know nothing about Medicine; if they did, you would soon have other news.

Alexander: High Potentates of Christendom have other things to do;

hence they have learned persons to serve and help them.

Bernhardus: Yes, certainly help them—from this life into the next. I could tell you something about Princes, did I not wish to spare the heads of those who have driven them from one illness into another, and, at last, even killed them. I myself have been present when a young prince was sick, and not knowing what to do, one of them said: Let us proceed according to the method and we shall be excused. How like you this advice? Your method must be right, should every prince give up the ghost under it. What says Paracelsus of the physicians of the Emperor and great lords? Does he not declare that they know less than peasants, rather helping their princes to death than to life, and that, having such physicians, it is impossible for them to reach old age? Have you never heard a prince lament: This multitude of physicians has destroyed me? Also, what said the Emperor Adrian when about to die?

The concourse of physicians frequently changes the Emperor! But what sort of doctors were these? Just the same whom the Burgomaster of Rome drove away and forbade the city. The truth about medicine was not discovered at that time, when the phantasy concerning humours was believed in.

Alexander: From the beginning of the world this Medicine has been held in high honour; that it should now be brought into contempt and replaced by another is difficult to believe.

Bernhardus: Adam, our first father, who had knowledge of all arts, also received that of Medicine from God, and it was kept secret by the learned (as the great gift of God) until Noah's time. When God destroyed the world by the Flood, the art of Medicine, with many other excellent arts, was lost. No one remained who knew them except Noah, called by some Hermogenes, or Hermes, to whom Antiquity ascribes the knowledge of all things celestial and terrestrial. The same Noah, before his death, described Medicine, skilfully concealing it among other matter. After his death this knowledge returned to God, and thus, through the Flood and Noah's death, was taken away from the Human Race.

Alexander: Who can believe God to have been so ungracious to man as to have taken from him this knowledge of Medicine?

Bernhardus: Tell me, does God think more of our Souls' salvation than that of our mortal bodies?

Alexander: Doubtless most of that of our Souls.

Bernhardus: Why, then, has He concealed Salvation during the 5,000 years before Christ was made man? When Christ was revealed to the world, then men heard the news of their Salvation, and there fell to the ground hundreds of idols, raised by men according to their own imaginations, although they knew not what was their souls salvation. For the notion of the Deity is naturally innate in man, which is even a better idea than knowledge; by which is incited the natural desire of good, reasoning, and judgment. Thus do idols spring from the imagination of men. And, forasmuch as human reason, the origin of philosophy, of which Erastus and writers of his stamp boast much in our time, need not necessarily be without deceit and guile, it has always fallen short of the truth until God assumed human reason through the mind, and His Word became flesh and man. It is not possible for our Reason—although mind—to grasp the Truth, until our intellect has been lighted by God's Word, and Reason receives Divine illumination through the mind, which then took place when the Word became flesh and dwelt in us. Before that time Theology was man's vain suppositions (I speak not of the few enlightened by God through the Holy Ghost before the Incarnate Word), and he understood not his soul's salvation. If God has concealed the same from humanity for 5,000 years, is it incredible that he should withhold the body's salvation — *i.e.*, Medicine — for 4,000 years?

Alexander: If Medicine, as you say, has only reappeared in our own time, whence comes the medicine which has been practised during the last 4,000 years?

Bernhardus: Whence came the idols which, before Christ, were in Europe, Africa, and Asia? Our human reason has speculated them out, and thus also has it happened with Medicine. After Noah's time, men, harrassed by diseases, sought refuge, one in herbs, another in animals, a third in stones and metals, and thus one thing after another was tried, without full knowledge of the same, which had some appearance of virtue. But there was as yet no doctor. The sick were carried to some public place, those who had had similar complaints shewing them the remedies used by themselves, which the patients tried on chance. Such was Medicine until the time of Apollo, *i.e.*, 1915 B.C.

This Apollo was a clever and learned man, and carefully noting those things which proved efficacious in diseases, he began to visit the sick, and thus became a public physician, to whom, after his death, a temple was erected and divine honours were paid. In such honour was Medicine then held which to-day begs its bread. Æsculapius succeeding his father, also treated the sick with skill and knowledge inherited from his father, and to him there was a temple erected, as to a god. After his death the kings commanded that all medical discoveries and observations should be written down and publicly exhibited on the walls of the Temple of Æsculapius. 457 years after came Hippocrates Cous, who was commanded to arrange the experiments in the Temple of Æsculapius, which he did; and, from these experiments, first invented methodical Medicine. Hence from him Medicine, as now taught in the schools, derives its origin. When Empirical Medicine thus came into great honour in Greece, many physicians arose, as Diocles, Chrysippus, Coristinus, Anaxagoras, Erostratus. 500 years after Hippocrates came Galenus, a plausible man who described the Hippocratic Medicine, painting it in beautiful colours, inventing causes and symptoms of diseases, ascribing virtues to herbs, and teaching the cure of feverish illnesses by cold, that of cold ones by heat. Thus did Human Speculation, from experiments, deduce the Science of Medicine—yet, at bottom, it was no Science, but mere opinions, accepted as Truth itself. But God, who is not always wrath with man, has, in our own time, chosen Philip Theophrastus Bombast, of Hohenheim, to rekindle the light of Medical Science, and to expose the deceit practised in his day. Therefore, this Theophrastus is the True Monarch of Medicine, and will remain so until the end of time. Therefore, it behoves us to thank God and his chosen man, and not lightly reject or revile what we do not understand. This science is above human knowledge, a gift and miracle of God. He errs that would grasp the same with human understanding, for, without the Revelation of the Holy Ghost and Inspiration of God, no one will obtain it—be he bachelor, master, or doctor.

Alexander: How can Paracelsus have rediscovered the true medicine, since he has written so many contradictory things about which his very disciples are not agreed? One says the Art is in Antimony, another in Mercury, Gold, Pearls, and Corals, or in Vitriol, Tartar, and many other poisonous things. that destroy men's lives. I know princes and lords who are terrified at the very mention of Paracelsian doctors.

Bernhardus: Only those who do not understand the writings of Paracelsus call them contradictory. But Holy Writ also must suffer the same imputation; as, for instance, Sebastian Franck exclaimed with regard to it: But is it true? However, I cannot deny that much is attributed to Paracelsus which he has never written. So also he himself, in a Theological Treatise, confesses that, in his youth, when seeking the first principles of Medicine, he had written things afterwards repudiated by himself, and doth warn us against the same, which (he says) had in time come to be accepted as true and perfect books. What you advance against his disciples is not the fault of Paracelsus. But what think you is the cause of their disagreement?

Alexander: I would hear it from you.

Bernhardus: You know that Christian Theology is one and united; whence come so many Sects among Christians in Europe?

Alexander: There have always been Sects in our Religion. I hold God permits this the better to prove the Righteous; but what has that to do with Medicine?

Bernhardus: The fact of there being so many heretics in our Religion is a sure sign and argument that the instigators of the Sects understand not Theology. Thus also in Medicine—the letter is the cause of all errors, yet no one will see that the letter is dead. What has Paracelsus written other than the letter, the right understanding of which comes from God? If it comes from ourselves, the Medical Heretics are there.

Alexander: Many laud Paracelsian Medicine. — Who shall say which of these understand Paracelsus aright?

Bernhardus: What says Christ, when asked by what false prophets shall be known?

Alexander: "By their fruits shall ye know them," Christ replied.

Bernhardus: Thus also shall a physician be discerned by his works, not words. By works Paracelsus proved that he had received Medicine from God, and was a physician born, whom also hypocrites hate.

Alexander: But what think you of the Medicine derived from the Experiments arranged and methodized by Hippocrates—is it good for nothing?

Bernhardus: I say not so; they are

to be praised who have made known to us herbs and natural simples. But philosophy is not necessary for the sick, as Serapion testifies. For the causes of serious diseases, as Apoplexy, Paralysis, Podagra, Dropsy, are all not natural but metaphysical, having their own Medicine as regards the fleshly body and vital parts, as heart, lungs, liver, etc., and for them Medicines enough are found—but what is taught concerning the causes of diseases is all mere opinion. Since Noah's time no one has understood the causes of so-called incurable diseases, but Paracelsus alone. Therefore, to Hippocrates and Galenus, but also to Paracelsus, let due praise be given according to the respective merit of each. With regard to the internal organization of man, Galenus was blind, as are also his disciples. Paracelsus has been the first *Medicus Microcosmi* (physician of man's body). Hence, he rightly calls himself *Monarchus Medicorum*, at which title Erastus the Calumniator is like to burst.

Alexander: Paracelsus ascribes the cause of diseases to the Stars, administering such poisonous Medicines against these Stars that the Galenian doctors are aghast.

Bernhardus: The inner man is astral, hence he must have astral Medicine. What Medicines have you in which there is not poison, of which people die who would otherwise live? Take, for instance, wine. Is that not a necessary and useful thing? And yet how great poison is there in it!

Alexander: Those who swill wine every day find no poison in it.

Bernhardus: They have to thank their strong constitution for that. When weakened they will soon find out whether there be poison in it. Know you not that the less poison there is, the less Medicine, and the stronger the poison, the stronger the Medicine. But you Galenians will not recognise poison, speaking of phlegma, melancholy, and cholera—wherein is nonsense—knowing not that the poison in medicine and food does everything.

Alexander: I have long noticed that the excrements of food and drink produce many diseases in us. Paracelsus has also written much concerning Tartar. But what the excrements in us are composed of, how they become a disease, what transmutes them into another substance, I know not, and cannot learn from his writings, much less understand the *fabricator* of the disease, the instrument with which it works, and the subject out of which it is made and multiplied.

Bernhardus: The true doctor must know more than of melancholy and cholera; with them the patient is not served. We, thank God, are better acquainted with man, and with what constitutes his sickness and health. Therefore we may well laugh at Erastus, Bernhardus Dessenius, Croneburgius, Lucas Stengeleinus, and other pseudo-doctors like them. Did not Christian love, and the misery and need of the sick, so compel us, we had rather be silent than mention the true Medicine to such blind, stubborn persons.

Alexander: It is our duty to assist our neighbour where we can. Medicine, which, next to God, should be man's refuge in sickness, is despised in our time. The peasants, observing that doctors understand it not, prefer to die than to entrust to them their bodies. Be not afraid because some rail at the truth. Help those who seek it. Let the choleric and melancholic dogs bark; they cannot harm you. Not everyone may understand the Truth, yet it must be taught, should but one in a thousand receive it. Therefore, for our old friendship's sake, I beg you to instruct me concerning the simples enumerated by Paracelsus in the chapter about Dropsy, what they are and where to be found. Also shew me how to get to the bottom of the matter, since Galenus knew the true cause of disease, and the Stars of Paracelsus are beyond me.

Bernhardus: Paracelsus prescribes three things for the cure of dropsy. The same cannot be explained in few words. Natural Magic is extinct in our day, hence also its terms are not understood. I will tell you as much as necessary for this time. In order that the ignorance of doctors concerning the cause of dropsy may be plainly shewn, let us examine the cure set up by Erastus in vol. iv. of his Disputations against Paracelsus! You will then perceive the hideous labyrinth of doctors, and what a coarse fellow Erastus is, wholly ignorant of man's creation and composition. Therefore, say on about what you would know; this afternoon I will devote to our colloquies, to-morrow I have other things to do. What says Paracelsus concerning the cure of dropsy?

Alexander: He divides the same into Diagnosis, Purgation, and Strengthening. The disease is to be resolved into water, without which it cannot be cured. But how shall the medicine resolve into water a disease consisting of water? I have myself seen more than a pailful of water taken from a dropsical patient. If the disease be water, what is to be digested?

Bernhardus: The water can and ought not to be digested, but that which is not yet water, and which clings to the nutriment of the blood. That is the excrement of food, called Tartar by Paracelsus. This Tartar is the disease to be resolved by digestion.

Alexander: How does this resolution take place?

Bernhardus: Through digestion.

Alexander: What is digestion?

Bernhardus: It is a medicinal power, separating Tartar from Nutriment, bad from good, disease from health. In this separation Tartar—which is a mucilage or viscous matter—melts into water. For Tartar in its first matter is nothing but water.

Alexander: In what form does this medical force act?

Bernhardus: Its action is like the Sun. Thus, Medicine is a Sun, and is called the Earthly Sun, or Sun of the Lower Firmament. That Tartar melts into water is well known to all experts in Natural Magic, but when melted in water it still remains Tartar, even as salt cast into water remains salt. Hence an Astrum (Star) must be there.

Alexander: What is an Astrum?

Bernhardus: That you will learn when we speak of Medicines to be taken from the excrement.

Alexander: I understand that the Tartaric Phlegm is the matter of disease, and that this phlegm is an excrement of food. Does this matter proceed alone from food?

Bernhardus: No; also from the air, poisoned by the vapours of the Earth, Water, or Firmament, which in us becomes a Tartar.

Alexander: Does Tartar come from every, or from one particular, food?

Bernhardus: Herein lies not a little philosophy. The Humorists are not worthy to learn it. However, I will discover to you somewhat of this secret.

The Tartar of dropsy is the excrement of various foods, as bread, fruit, and all kinds of roots and herbs. This Tartar is, in its essence, cold.

Alexander: How should this Tartar be cold when we in preparing it see that it is nothing but water, and sharper, more burning, than salt?

Bernhardus: Every essence is water, and externally hot from the resolution of the elemental body; therefore this Tartar is cold fire. Now, these Tartars which come into us through meat and drink are divided into four genera. One kind is in the fruits of the earth; another in the food obtained from water, such as fish, etc. The third is in the flesh of animals and birds. The fourth is from the firmament. Each kind has its place in the body which it possesses. Had philosophers rightly apprehended these excrements, Melancholy and Cholera had never been imported into Medicine. They were good, lazy fathers, judging things by externals. It is not written on everyone's forehead what in him is.

Virtue must be known *ex radice centri*, not by its superficies.

Alexander: Can one detect the kind of Tartar present in the patient, or must it be assumed?

Bernhardus: In Medicine what cannot be understood should not be assumed, for Medicine is subject to its works, as Theology to Faith, which, however, must be confirmed by works.

Alexander: Where does one find the Tartar of Disease? Is it found in Urine?

Bernhardus: It is present in Urine, but is imperceptible.

Alexander: Why?

Bernhardus: In Urine there is not Tartar alone, but many other things in which Tartar lies hidden.

Alexander: How is it detected in Urine?

Bernhardus: The art of separation distinguishes the parts from one another, viz., *Fumus Salis* (Smoke of Salt), called gore by Paracelsus; water from the food; superfluous salt; Sulphur; finally we find Tartar in its four kinds. He who can distinguish them perceives of what kind the Tartarus Morbi is.

Alexander: I have never heard of this separation, nor do I know how it is done, but I admit that this art is most necessary to a physician.

Bernhardus: He who is unacquainted therewith will remain a Melancholic or Choleric doctor, for he cannot thoroughly understand the matter of the disease, and therefore it is impossible for him to know wherewith the "fabricator of diseases" plagues us, breaking the machine of the Lesser World (human body) and driving out life. Now, no one can deny that Galenus, Avicenna, and all other doctors writing before Paracelsus, knew nothing of this Tartar, and a clever physician of Heidelberg would be equally ignorant. It is a great impertinence to be-little a thing one does not understand. It is just as if a cobbler wished to teach a tailor his trade. I tell you that he who can find and judge this Tartar in Urine is more worthy in Medicine than if the four volumes written by Erastus against Paracelsus had wiped his posterior extremities. I mention not other secrets far greater than this.

Alexander: You said just now that each genus of Tartar possesses a particular portion of the human body. In what part is the Tartar we are now speaking about?

Bernhardus: In the part subject to Venus and Mars.

Alexander: What and whence is this philosophy? I have never yet heard of this phantasy.

Bernhardus: I believe you. Had you attended the School of Physic as long as that of Sophistry, you would not call it phantasy.

Alexander: How shall I understand this?

Bernhardus: Those are the places within us in which the spirits of the kidneys, mother, and gall rejoice and exult.

Alexander: The astronomers say

dropsy comes from Saturn. What did you say about Venus and Mars?

Bernhardus: Although some astronomers subject dropsy to Mars, yet Saturn is the cause of disease when we come to the cause. I speak here not of the cause, but place.

Alexander: What is the place *(locus)*?

Bernhardus: Open your eyes and search in Astronomy, and you will find it—also from the following description—

Alexander: Before proceeding to the means of cure, tell me, are there other excrements in food and drink besides Tartar?

Bernhardus: Food and drink have three excrements, viz., (1) Water, (2) Salt or Tartar, (3) Sulphur.

Alexander: I understand the water. But what are Salt and Sulphur?

Bernhardus: Salt is the earth found in every creature. Sulphur is a solid, burning when cast into fire, and is the fire in wood, in fishes, in flesh, in stones, in metals.

Alexander: According to Paracelsus, there are in a body not more than three substances, Mercury, Sulphur, and Salt. You say they are excrements. If there be but these three in food, what then is nutriment?

Bernhardus: Now you ask me not a little thing. Rather tell me from Galenus what nutriment is.

Alexander: What should it be but the most subtle and purest (essence) in food, which "is assimilated to the body," as Galenus says.

Bernhardus: A peasant, not a doctor, might put it so.

Alexander: One must speak according to one's understanding.

Bernhardus: Behold, is it not lamentable that all the lot of you know not what becomes flesh and blood in us? Why speak you of diseases and their origin, not knowing the least thing in Physics? All your writing and chatter is nought but a plausible deceit; how long have you befooled us! Think you, the world will always remain blind? O excellent men, that have not yet learnt the alphabet of Medicine, not to speak of anything more! Shame on you for opening your reviling mouths against the beloved man through whom God has restored to us the Science of Medicine! What would you say to a cobbler, boasting he could make the best shoes and never having seen the leather they are made of? Would you not rebuke him? What shall be said of you, writing great books and chattering in your lecture-rooms? It is easy to preach about colours to the blind. You have never seen Medicine, and know not whether it be black or blue. I speak here of the Science of Medicine, not of local remedies—called by you specifics—that is, of things good for stomach, liver, etc., etc., aperients and so forth. These are not the things that dignify the physician, and whence he has his name. But you have set your specifics in the place of Medicine, and adulterated them by your own compositions. Is it not true that the Sisters of Ulm restore more sick persons with their specifics, than you by your method?

Alexander: I know Princes of the Empire who have been treated and cured by Galenian doctors.

Bernhardus: They use the Simples as given by God. What the doctor and apothecary concoct often does more harm than good. But one dare not say so for fear of being called an idiot. Both are most honourable gentlemen who would fain blind those that see. Yet their wise Worships know not what is the nutriment in bread and wine. But, not knowing this, you also know not what are excrements, and what is the matter of many diseases. You see there must be something, you know not what, and therefore it must be Cholera, Melancholy, Phlegm, or Blood. Were you skilled in Physics, you would therein find—not Cholera and Melancholy—but excrements, comprised by Paracelsus under the name of Tartar. But, being ignorant of Tartar, you know not on what the Medicine must act, nor what that is which separates Tartar from Nutriment. Hence, as you will hear, the Resolution of Tartar is a mystery. I have thus described Tartar, what it is, into how many kinds divided—to which certainly dropsy belongs—that you may understand Paracelsus's saying: Dropsy arises not from the element Water, but from the Earth.

Alexander: I have often wondered at that saying since the disease is dropsy. Now, I see that Tartar—the disease in man—proceeds from the products of the earth used as food by him. But I should have thought that our nature would remove the excrements and feces.

Bernhardus: That it does when well, but when infected, or impeded by outward accident, it cannot perform its office, and the excrements remain in the chyle. Hence in stomach and liver proceed stomach and liver complaints, in the kidneys diabetes, calculus, putrefactions, in the joints Podagra, Arthetica, &c.

Alexander: Is everything we eat and drink mingled with these excrements, *i.e.*, Tartar?

Bernhardus: Everything. God has so ordered it that no food is free from this poison.

Alexander: Can the excrements be separated from food outside of man's body?

Bernhardus: The grossest can be separated, viz., those falling out of the stomach into the intestines — not the others. Hence also the juice of herbs should be extracted, the rest thrown away. Look at rectified spirits, how subtle they are, yet in them is still the Tartar which Nature alone separates This Tartar, by reason of its subtlety, is most similar to Tartar of the Firmament, a strong kind, whence arise plague, pleurisy, and various fevers.

Alexander: Is the water in dropsical patients resolved Tartar?

Bernhardus: In a patient who has been tapped, and in whom the water reappears not, in that water is resolved

Tartar. But where the water reappears in the patient, the Tartar remains in him.

Alexander: But what is the water?

Bernhardus: Our blood and flesh, and the nutriment from the food, together with its liquid excrement.

Alexander: How are these changed into water?

Bernhardus: Through water. Thus, in Tartar is (1) its own Elemental Water, (2) the Astral Water which is the cause of disease. These two waters unite in Tartar, like male and female semen, producing a poison fatal to our flesh and blood.

Alexander: How is this fatal result produced?

Bernhardus: The Salt in flesh and blood being the medium of the other two, when the former is in health flesh and blood remain whole; on the separation of salt destruction begins. The same can be converted into all kinds of salts. According to the transmutation is the disease. Thus, in dropsy, the microcosmic salt is melted, by the above poisons, to water; now flesh and blood lose their being, and are changed into water, their primary matter. The Nutriment (which is not yet blood) is not water, but a viscous liquor, a medium between primary and final matter, *i.e.*, between water and blood, or flesh, or whatever else was to become of the Nutriment. This medium is also resolved into water.

Alexander: How comes it that Nature resolves some Tartars, driving them out with the water, and others not?

Bernhardus: In the Tartar resolvable by Nature, the elemental poison alone does the mischief. This your laxatives and herbs may expel. Hence you may cure such dropsy. But when the elemental poison is united to the firmamental, then Nature's laxatives have no power, and—the water reappearing after tapping—you call the disease incurable. Hence it is evident that you understand not medicine and the causes of diseases.

Alexander: I have seen some dropsical patients cured, and also many die. Now, I understand that elemental diseases are cured with elemental Medicines. But firmamental ones alone with firmamental remedies, of which we Galenians know nothing. I understand also what Paracelsus calls elemental disease. I would know something more concerning Tartar before we come to the Medicine for Tartar.

Bernhardus: How can I treat of all the mysteries of Tartar in a single disease? Tartar is a wonderful creation of God's—in it is the mother of all creatures. The upper Heaven procreates from it wondrous things on earth, the *Astra Microcosmi* (stars of the lesser world, *i.e.*, human body), many diseases, of which I will now say nothing. Would that physicians knew Tartar—not only its transmutations in food and drink—but also what God has created from it in Nature! They would then behold great wonders, daily before our eyes but not recognised. Hence many despise Paracelsus's writings through ignorance, not knowing Tartar more than the peasant who says Tartar is the crust in wine barrels. The time has come when this, and other, blindness must be exposed, to the praise of God and weal of the sick.

Alexander: In future I will pay more attention to Tartar and its diseases. Tell me, now, how is it resolved and expelled?

Bernhardus: Paracelsus names two Medicines, an external and an internal one. The former is to digest, mature, and resolve the disease, expelling the inward, viscous Tartar.

Alexander: He says the Medicines to expel Tartar are dung, and come from dung, as: Columbinum and Gallinaceum; what these things are I know not, *e.g.*, Rebis!

Bernhardus: The learned are wont, when treating of Nature's secrets, to wrap up the truth in other matter. Here he gives the Medicine its right name, *i.e.*, Rebis, adding Columbinum and Gallinaceum to mislead his enemies.

Alexander: I doubt whether external poultices are able to resolve Tartar, which lies so deep in the body.

Bernhardus: Poultices, liniments, etc., are not to be rejected; although they resolve not the Tartar, they promote the action of the Medicine.

Alexander: Must Rebis be applied externally, like Gallinaceum and Columbinum?

Bernhardus· Know that man is divided into inner and outer man. Each has its Medicine, and, since the outer man is but dust and ashes, and of a like nature is the *Materia Morbi* which plagues us, so also must the Medicine consist of things similar to these—called by Paracelsus *stercora* (filth). Not that the Medicine is filth, but it arises in filth, as the inner in the outer man; and, even as death divides the inner and outer man, so does art separate Medicine from filth.

Alexander: What is this dung from which the Medicine to cure Tartar is taken?

Bernhardus: You may learn this from Paracelsus, who says: External and Internal Medicine are similar; both have a head; one helps the other. From these words it follows that Columbinum and Gallinaceum are not the external Medicine, for, how are they similar to Mercury? and how have they a head?

Alexander: I don't know what he calls Mercury. Mercury is commonly called Quicksilver.

Bernhardus: Mercury is a general term; it exists in all creatures, and is water.

Alexander: Here he means metallic Mercury.

Bernhardus: Not at all, although it may appear so. That is not our Mercury which is found in Quicksilver and all other metals. The matter (primary) of Quicksilver and metals is water—frozen water, like crystal. Thus, also, there is water in metals. A mineral, sulphureous, igneous Spirit pervades this water and transmutes it into a metal.

Chemists call it generating spirit, and say: Dry water and the generating spirit are Nature's principles.

Alexander: I see I must have a better knowledge of metals to thoroughly understand this Mercury.

Bernhardus: Many, both Ancients and Moderns, have written about the metals. Read them.

Alexander: I have read them long ago. They differ. I fancy they have had but little experience. By reading and speculation Truth cannot be attained. Seeing and handling is necessary. You have seen and experienced a resolution of metals. Hence you can inform me correctly. Seeing is Believing! As the Proverb says: The ocular witness of one is better than the hearsay evidence of ten.

Bernhardus: I admit you cannot discover the truth about Tartar without knowing what Mercury is. But what shall I tell you about secrets which are said to be unfathomable?

Alexander: Let a thing be hidden

ever so long, it must come to light at last.

Bernhardus: It is said: Time brings Roses. Time also reveals Nature's secrets. Time has given me knowledge which I will here impart to you. Basel, Cologne, Denmark, Silesia, and where else the great Paracelsian doctors dwell, wish to reveal nothing before the time. I like not these long prefaces. They affirm that our Autumn is not yet come, and therefore are our fruits sour. That is not bringing Paracelsian Medicine to light.

Alexander: I have heard many learned men say the same.

Bernhardus: Wherefore much talk and no instruction. Who would guess we had tasted a drop of Paracelsian Truth?

Alexander: I should think more highly of it, were the students first taught the right foundation on which Occult Medicine stands. But one chatters of Antimony, another of Gold, Pearls, Coral, etc. I know Antimony is a strong emetic and purgative, as also Hellebore. I know that Pearls comfort, as also Melissa, Crocus, etc. Here in dropsy Mercury cures, but so also does Coloquint. Although I am acquainted with this, yet my knowledge is no knowledge, since I am ignorant of the basis and cause. Hence those who are instructed should lecture and write concerning the foundation, that young doctors might understand Paracelsus' books. If that be not done, the Paracelsian tree, which began to flourish Anno '58, will bear no fruit for many years.

Bernhardus: You are right. Our opponents believe us to have no other foundation than what we know concerning the three principles, S., Sulphur, and Salt. But these learned gentlemen are so misled by their envy and hatred, that they judge of unknown matters as a blind man of colours. The lost art of Medicine—recovered by Paracelsus—had an eternally sure foundation, against which all the gates of Hell cannot prevail, let alone the trashy books which

Erastus, with his blind, stubborn adherents, has vomited forth against God and the truth. The true principles will remain as we teach them, but it is untrue to say they are our foundation. I well know this house stands on the earth, and the earth is its foundation. But what the earth stands on, and what its foundation is, every peasant does not know, also not Dr. Förtyle at Heidelberg, although he be a good Dialectician and Rhetorician, and well read in Aristotle. He who is acquainted with the basis of our three principles, knows our foundation, not Galenus and his spawn, Erastus. Be not surprised that many followers of Paracelsus are ignorant of this foundation. Remember rather the text: "Many are called, but few chosen." Medicine comes not from seeing and hearing, or much reading, but from God, through inspiration of the Holy Spirit. It is in God, and comes from Him. From Him we should speak and write, not from ink and paper, as many of our followers do.

Alexander: I have read in Paracelsus that many would adopt his practice, did he not beg them not to attempt this until after long experience.

Bernhardus: We wish to fly before the time, hence we must drown with Cato in the deep sea. What think you, who shall explain the mysteries of Paracelsus? Truly we consider ourselves great philosophers, and yet our knowledge is nothing but vanity. Hence the proverb: The world is ruled by opinions. The present time is not ripe for the knowledge of these mysteries, for it has never tasted rest. When the time comes—before the Day of Judgment—in which the secrets of all hearts are laid bare, at that time, says Paracelsus: I order my writings to be judged.

Alexander: I understand not this passage concerning rest. Be that as it may, I know neither doctor nor master is born so. All must be learnt. In this is labour and trouble until one has understood what one would learn. Then one has rest from learning.

Bernhardus: Happy he who is at rest. He has conquered all labour and trouble. He now lives in knowledge; therein his heart abides, which in time was troubled and bound fast in woes. The physician must be at rest who would expound Paracelsus to youth. Whether the doctor is at rest who spends much time in preparing Vitriol and Tartar, I leave to the judgment of every learned man. Our aim should be a very different one. Hence you must not take my speaking of these things in a manner beyond your comprehension amiss. What I know of these secrets I have acquired with great pains and labour.

Alexander: I would have instruction from your experience, not from this or that author. When we were young comrades in Italy you would be subject to no sect, but you said with Horace:

A stranger I, whithersoever the winds may bear me;
No lord claims my allegiance.

Hence I would listen to your views, not those of Galenus or of any other contained in Books and Writings.

Bernhardus: It would not be easy to do without books; but what is contained and hidden in books can only be expounded by those who have penetrated into the hidden meaning and spirit of the same. We all know that our Christian New Testament has been written by men full of the Holy Ghost. But when men, possessing little of the Holy Spirit and much of their own, approach these mysteries, what harm and trouble they cause in the world! Thus also must happen, in our Faculty, to those who—knowing how to prepare Oil of Mercury or Vitriol, etc.—would meddle with the medicine of Paracelsus. Hence I would beg every reasonable man not to attempt to discover the mysteries of Medicine with such vain and mechanical work, but to reflect on the names of the mysteries, what Oil of Mercury, Juice of Coral, Resin of Gold, really mean, for they must not be taken literally. Behold the disciples of Galenus, how many thousand books they have made out of a single one of his! Were we to do so, the literature of Paracelsus would soon grow up.

Alexander: I believe Galenus is easier to understand than Paracelsus; hence easier to write about.

Bernhardus: What he says concerning the properties of Simples is plain. Also his phantasies concerning these properties are not hard to grasp. But it is different with the Books of Paracelsus. He writes concerning Nature's Secrets and God's Wondrous Works. Everyone cannot understand, nor write about, these. They must, indeed, be simpletons who imagine that *Tartarus Auri* is gold, *Mercurius precipitatus* quicksilver, etc. They give it to patients, saying they have it from Paracelsus, an excellent physician. O, you simpletons! These are secrets only to be understood by those who have received understanding from above. Hence no one will do much with Tincture of Mercury, Potable Gold, etc., until he has discovered their real signification. Since you also regard Science more for use and profit than for her own sake, think not that God will grant your wish! Therefore, I again beg of those called to these things to leave details and seek the foundation. They will thus gain a knowledge of the mysteries requisite for expounding the Books of Paracelsus, which should not continue in darkness, but be explained by us I will be the first to tread this path, and, in the due measure that He shall grant me knowledge, so shall I interpret the same.

Alexander: A Parisian doctor, L. G. (calling himself Leo Suavius), has written a treatise on the Book *De Vita Longa*. How like you his interpretation of Paracelsus' terms? He finds no difficulty in common names like Mercury, Vitriol, etc.; hence, I suspect, he has not yet discovered the secrets of Medicine.

Bernhardus: This good Leo Suavius has wished to communicate to others his opinion, derived from a study of Paracelsus, for them to accept or reject according to their own private judgment. He has made the first attempt to expound the magic words in Paracelsus. For this he is to be praised, but no one is bound by his opinion. As regards Medical Simples, perhaps he has never tried them, and believes the same to possess the virtues described by Paracelsus.

Alexander: I used to think in this way. Now I find it is different. Mercury puzzled me much before I found out that a secret was contained in the name. Some days ago I read in a Treatise (by Castner, of Hamburg) that Mercury is an Arcanum the like of which the world cannot shew. Hence, I would fain know what it is.

Bernhardus: To come to the point! Listen to what I am about to say! You are a Chemist, and skilled in experimental work. Hence you will easily understand me. Had you been an armchair doctor, my speech would sound strange in your ears. Therefore will I here speak to you and your like, yet, not otherwise or farther than is meet, and God's Word permits. What says Paracelsus of Mercury in that Chapter?

Alexander: That it is the internal Medicine, having power to expel the resolved Salt. It is to be separated from its ore when dead, for when dead it is Mercury, when living Quicksilver.

Bernhardus: How understand you this preparation?

Alexander: Mercury—*i.e.*, Quicksilver—is to be extracted from its ore, and a precipitate made from it with Hydrochloric Acid.

Bernhardus: What is the ore of Mercury?

Alexander: Red mineral earth. Some call it Cinnabar; some say it is the Minium of the Ancients.

Bernhardus: When Mercury is extracted from this ore, is it dead or living?

Alexander: Living.

Bernhardus: Is it living in the ore, or is it made living by melting?

Alexander: Water makes it not alive, hence it is so created in the ore.

Bernhardus: Behold Paracelsus speaks not of such Mercury, but of that which in its ore is dead. Extraction from the ore neither kills it nor makes it alive. Hence it must be either dead or living in the ore. The Mercury we mean must be dead, not living. Is not Erastus ashamed to accuse Paracelsus of purging dropsy with Hydrargyrum (Mercury), since Paracelsus publicly says it is the dead Mercury; speaking not of Hydrargyrum, *i.e.*, Quicksilver—as Erastus lies—but of Mercury, which is no Hydrargyrum?

Alexander: Erastus, like others, thinks Mercury is Quicksilver.

Bernhardus: Erastus, who sets up for a learned man, ought to understand this matter better than common people, ignorant of letters and science. For those who wander about, boasting of great arts, and promising to enrich others, whilst they are themselves beggars, are commonly a low sort. One is a goldsmith, another a tailor, a third a cobbler, or runaway monk, or student.

Some know a little Latin, some none at all.

Alexander: Such artists have often caused me much loss.

Bernhardus: It serves you and all others right, who think to discover the great mysteries of God from such indifferent folk.

Alexander: Although they be unlearned, God often gives more grace to simple, common folk, than to the literate. It has often so happened. God's grace is not restricted. He is a Searcher of hearts, and according to them does He shew His mercy, not according to external appearance, which we men alone regard.

Bernhardus: I have never seen roast pigeons fly into anyone's mouth. When God gives understanding and grace in Magical Mysteries, He also gives understanding in other Sciences belonging to Magic. One finds not understanding with such people, let them therefore not boast of Grace! They poke about in Alchemistic books, saying Mercury is Quicksilver—to be calcinated in Aquafortis, precipitate—or boiled for four weeks with gold in a phial. Then it is an excellent medicine for all diseases, *aurum vitæ!* Such a philosopher is Erastus (he did not get much from Paracelsus), who gave Oil of Vitriol to his Excellency Councillor D. Alesius, thus sacrificing his life.

Alexander: He is a right learned man; the world has not his like; it is meet that he be spoken of respectfully; for he is a professor at Heidelberg, is well read in Zwinglius and Arrius. But what do I hear? Does he use Vitriol? I have never found any good in it. The Abbot of Fulda died of it. It ran through his penis into the bed and burned the sheets. I have also heard of a Queen who died shortly after it was given her by the physician.

Bernhardus: He has killed the good Alesius with it, and also others whose names I will not mention.

Alexander: Since he uses the Simples of Paracelsus, why is he so bitter, writing so many lies against him?

Bernhardus: Paracelsus has no greater enemies than the Galenian doctors, who think that they have only to look at a book to know the contents thereof. But the learned asses reflect not that Paracelsus wrote in the Magic style. Hence their brain is so full of raillery that Magic knowledge cannot enter. Therefore they cry: "Magic is Sorcery! Beware, it is the devil's work!" Whereas Magic is no Sorcery, but the greatest wisdom in God's works, and a penetrating into Occult Nature. So Erastus has read much of Oil of Vitriol! He understands not more than a layman, who knows that Vitriol is Copperas. Forsooth, a fine doctor! With respect to Mercury, he pretends Paracelsus means Quicksilver thereby, although he must have read in "The Book concerning the disease of the Gall" how violently Paracelsus wrote against Mercury.

Alexander: I know all, and think not other than that Mercury is Quicksilver. But Paracelsus might have prepared it medicinally so as to neutralise the poison.

Bernhardus: He is publicly against it in the "Book concerning Consumption."

Alexander: Since Mercury is nothing but Quicksilver, why does he use the name?

Bernhardus: Why call a thing other than it is?

Alexander: We know that gold is killed Quicksilver, and Quicksilver living gold, but, when speaking of gold, we call it gold and not Quicksilver. If Paracelsus did the same we should know what he meant.

Bernhardus: The Ancient Philosophers have named this matter Mercury; Paracelsus has retained the same, writing not for the common people but for philosophers.

Alexander: Who are the philosophers?

Bernhardus: Those who know Nature better than bookworms. A

Philosopher, hearing the name of Mercury, knows what it is; but he who knows not, holding Mercury of physicians to be Quicksilver, is a Sophist. Hence, Erastus is a Sophist, not having even learnt what Mercury is; but he is proud of knowing Greek, and that he can speak of Hydrargyrum. Paracelsus says in many places that Mercury is not Quicksilver. Erastus has doubtless seen this, but suppresses the fact in order to prejudice Paracelsus. Here the reasonable man perceives why Erastus and his like rage against Paracelsus. The devil seeks ways and means to preserve his Kingdom in this world. But, as the Apostle says, when perfection comes imperfection will be destroyed. This will also happen here when all sects shall be annihilated.

Alexander: Has Paracelsus not made Medicine from Quicksilver? What else is the Mercury of which he writes in this Chapter?

Bernhardus: Just the same of which he says that it lies in the ore and is separated from the same, dead.

Alexander: What is the ore?

Bernhardus: A mineral in which Philosophers' Mercury has been created by God.

Alexander: I had thought Philosophers' Mercury was artificial, and you say God has created it.

Bernhardus: God has created Mercury like other creatures. Art can do no more than extract and separate Mercury from its ore. Although God has created it, He has also created the physician who converts it into Medicine. For as it is found it is rather a poison than a Medicine. Hence the physician should know the art of separating the poison from the Medicine. Paracelsus here speaks of this separation, saying it is to be separated dead from its ore, for dead it is Mercury, but living Quicksilver.

Alexander: Quicksilver has also an ore from which it is extracted. Does Paracelsus mean this ore or another?

Bernhardus: In the ore of Quicksilver there is not the Sulphuric Spirit which kills Quicksilver; therefore he does not mean the same ore.

Alexander: Gold, Silver, Copper, Iron, Tin, Lead, all come from ores, each metal having its own ore in which Quicksilver is dead. Does he understand these ores to be the ores from which Mercury is to be extracted?

Bernhardus: No. For metal-yielding ores possess not the Mercurial Sulphuric Spirit, but that of their respective metals Paracelsus speaks here of the Quicksilver of Mercury, *i.e.*, of the Quicksilver by which Sulphur of Mercury is killed.

Alexander: I know no other Sulphur which kills Quicksilver but the Sulphur which is in the ore of metals.

Bernhardus: Hence you have paid but little attention to this passage in Paracelsus. Take and read the paragraph. What say you to it now?

Alexander: I had not looked for

Mercury here; I have often read the passage, but skipped over it.

Bernhardus: Have you not read in Alchemistic books that there is a medium between Mercury of the metals and common Mercury?

Alexander: I have never seen it expressly stated that the medium Mercury is to be found in this ore.

Bernhardus: The reason for this is because there is in this ore much poison which, used by those ignorant of Alchemistic processes, might do serious harm to the sick. Hence it is not to be called by its name.

Alexander: I know many Alchemists who prepare this Medicine, but all differently. Some use it for physic, others wish to make Gold and Silver of it.

Bernhardus: There is a great art in its preparation. First, it must be separated pure from its ore, and then digested in its full strength. This digestion is known to very few of those even who can separate it from its ore. Before digestion it is crude Mercury, and the crudity is poison, of which beware. When I first discovered the way of separating this Mercury from the ore, I thought nothing more was wanting. But, from experiments, I found it to be crude Mercury, and that I had not penetrated into its Arcanum.

Alexander: Although I have never attempted the separation from the ore, I see that this can be done. But how it is afterwards to be digested and brought to perfection I know not.

Bernhardus: This digestion is effected only by the Tincture of Sun and Moon, which digests not this Mercury alone, but transmutes all other metals and expels their poison.

Alexander: These tinctures are beyond my comprehension—much has been written concerning them, but, methinks, by those who have never set eyes on them. I do not see how a physician in our time is to have these tinctures and perfect medicines therewith, seeing that few know more about them than about the Mercury of Paracelsus.

Bernhardus: The tinctures cannot be spoken of too highly, but they can be easily understood by those who rightly use their understanding. But we are lunatic Alchemists, as Paracelsus says, threshing empty straw. God has given the tincture to the physician to purify unclean things, to transmute them into gold, and to expel from men all diseases arising from the influences of the stars. Hence it purifies not alone metals but also our blood. For it is the very essence of our life and the Anatomy in the Greater World—an eternal unquenchable fire—*ignis non urens, ignis cœlestis*—fructifying all things, restoring the dead to life. I will inform you further of these tinctures when treating of the Sun mentioned in this chapter. Here you shall learn of the dead Mercury, which is to be digested by these tinctures after separation from the ore. The same is the medicine which administered in dropsy expels the resolved salt. The other two medicines, viz.:—the Element Water and the Sun, shall be explained afterwards.

Alexander: Therefore this Mercury is to be our purge, expelling water in dropsy.

Bernhardus: Before the water overflows the heart. It is to be administered when the influence is greatest, *i.e.*, when the dropsical stone is in its greatest virulence.

Alexander: But—if I understand this passage aright—not purgation, but digestion by external medicine must take place. I will ask you concerning the external medicine later on. Please inform me now more fully concerning the generation of Mercury.

Bernhardus: Much has been written concerning this generation (as usual in our time) by those knowing little about it. But occult things are not to be fathomed by speculation, but by experience in the Art of Alchemy. Hence their writings are nothing but a misleading of youths who trust in them.

Alexander: I cannot sufficiently

lament the labyrinth such books have led me into.

Bernhardus: Concerning the name Mercury, know that it is a matter of Gold, Silver, and of all the other metals. But the understanding of this is not according to the letter, especially not as regards our laxative Mercury. It is not a component of metals, but that which it was before its heaven—*i.e.*, Sulphur—decocted and prepared it in its ore, the same is the substance and matter of all metals.

Alexander: The philosophers say all metals are formed from Quicksilver.

Bernhardus: That is false, for Quicksilver is a metal in gold as well as in silver, etc. But since it is living, it is not reckoned a metal in Adept Philosophy.

Alexander: Since Mercury is the matter of metals, as you have just said, what sort of thing is Mercury?

Bernhardus: Just the same as the substance out of which Quicksilver, Gold, Silver, Lead, Copper, etc., and our Medical Mercury, are made.

Alexander: Has this matter no name?

Bernhardus: The inventors of this Art have named it Mercury. Their successors—interpreting Magic literally—have supposed Mercury to be nothing but Quicksilver, which is the opinion of all book sages to this day.

Alexander: This matter must doubtless be in minerals. Paracelsus says metals are formed from water—is it water?

Bernhardus: All these things are of water. But water is the first matter—and the most remote—of metals.

Alexander: What is mediate, and immediate, matter?

Bernhardus: Although one should not speak more clearly concerning these things than is taught in Magical books, yet—since some of these books treating of this generation have doubtless been lost—I consider it necessary to explain this matter to preserve youth from false Alchemists. Therefore, listen.

Alexander: I have occupied myself much with Alchemistic books, but have never found that they inform us concerning the origin of metals. I have therefore lately concluded that it is all trash.

Bernhardus: The same was my experience when trusting to books. But when I found it different in water, I let Aristotle, Albertus, and his like be, and followed after truth, of which I thought more than all their books. You will also understand this secret by paying attention. The primary matter of Quicksilver and of all metals is, in the beginning, as an oil growing out of saltpetre in the hills. Now, all salts are nothing but water mixed with a little earth, which earth gives the water a taste. For according to the kind of earth is the taste of the salts. There is one kind of earth in common salt, another in saltpetre, another in vitriol, another in alumina, etc. In dissolving salts these earths are found and become visible. The salt growing out of saltpetre is dry, melts not when thrown into water, but is like glass or crystal. Chemists call this Mercurial Salt. Albertus was of opinion that the white earth in alum was most nearly related to this Mercury. But that cannot be, for aluminous earth has the nature of salts, but Mercurial earth that of stones. Mercury is composed of two things, water and earth.

Alexander: You mean here common water?

Bernhardus: Nothing else. But the earth is not common earth; it is the subtlest and purest of elements. It has many names which are daily in our mouths. But none save the Magus knows its true name. I should like to explain to you somewhat of this mystery, but you are too deep in the letter which blinds your eyes. Yet at the time of the New Birth I will not forget you. Understand that this earth is the subject into which flow all the influences of the whole firmament, the powers, virtues, and action of all the stars, an eternal dwelling of all heavenly spirits, bad and good, sweet and sour, black and white, not alone the subject of all metallic forms, but also of all mineral ones in all things created by God under the Moon's orb. Now, I will speak here of metals alone to the exclusion of other things.

EXTRACTS FROM THE BOOK OF THE THREE FACULTIES.

By Alexander von Suchten.

TO come at once to the point, I will begin by saying that the nearer man was to the Creation of the World the greater was his desire for a knowledge of Him who had created him, with Heaven and Earth, and all that therein is.

This desire was so strong that it left him no peace until he had found what he sought. At that time there was neither Theology, nor Astronomy, nor Medicine. Man knew no more than he had heard from his father Adam, how he had been created by God and placed in Paradise, had sinned therein, and had been expelled therefrom into the trouble and misery of this world.

How, then, should man know his Creator? In Heaven God was far removed from mortal eyes. Man could not behold Him in flesh and yet live. What should he do to find his Creator? Whilst meditating thus he observed—doubtless by Divine inspiration—that the Master can be recognised by His Masterpiece, in the great world and the little world (which is man) made out of the great world—or rather taken from and separated from it. Thus, man acknowledged the Master in His works in that great world wherein he saw a small grain grow into a great tree. He reflected further that the world must once have been different from what it now is, and that the seed grain which grows into a tree must once have been something else than a grain. He could not understand these things with his human reason, but continued to seek, and invented many arts, among them the "Art of Water." For he beheld how everything was, by fire, destroyed and reduced to what it had been, *i.e.*, to earth. He therefore thought of separating things by means of water, not to destroy them, but to see whether hidden properties might be revealed to him by this separation. Thus, after much pains, he at length discovered the *Art of Separation.* Then he wished to know how everything in the great world was put together, and so divided that world into three parts— Animals, Vegetables, and Minerals, *i.e.*, one part he gave to the animals; the second to things growing out of the earth; the third to things growing under the earth. Then he began diligently to investigate one class after another. Man he assumed to be the noblest and most intelligent creature of God. By farther using his Art of Separation, and by comparing one thing with another, he found that the primary matter of man and the primary matter of the great world are one and the same thing.

But this primary matter of the world and of man is a Crystalline

Water, of which Holy Writ says:—"Before God created Heaven and Earth, the Spirit of the Lord brooded over the Waters." Thus water became a primary matter of both. But where remains the Spirit of the Lord, which brooded over the waters, after the two worlds, *i.e.*, heaven, and earth, and man had been created from the same? I reply, in the primary matter of man and of the world. God, who is Perfection, has wished to dwell in man. But here the following question might be put: how did man know—since the primary matter of man and of the world is a crystalline water—how could man know whether the Spirit of the Lord had remained in this primary matter of the world, or of man? I reply, he knew it by the Art of Water, for Water was his teacher. This teacher shewed him how the world dies, how the Spirit departs from it, how the body is without Spirit, the Spirit without body. He saw how the Spirit returns to the body, and the body revives. He saw by the decay of the world that it did not become again what it had been before. Hence it became plain to him that God dwells not in that which passes away, but in that which is Eternal.

Thus far I have recorded (1) how God Almighty in the beginning created two things: the Great and the Small World; (2) How man was taken from the Great World and became a separate world; (3) How he discovered the Art of Water and learnt what was the primary matter of both Greater and Lesser World; (4) The qualities of each; (5) How the world is temporal—man eternal.

Now I will speak of the things arising from the water—*i.e.*, primary matter, as well as how the first man discovered and divided them, taught them to his children, and described them.

But this I write from my experience, of which alone I make use, and of the Spirit given me by God. Did

I write from Theology, Astronomy, or Medicine, I should have to employ their respective terms. But I am here teaching according to the rules of no special art, but according to that Art which was before them all, and is the mother of them all, *i.e.*, Magic, which in our time has gone into exile, and lies hidden, God knows where, but is quite unknown to men who, relying upon their understanding as upon the Holy Ghost, exalt themselves like Lucifer against heaven. But, banished from before God's face for our pride, we may one day confess that our human intellect is naught, that by the same we cause ourselves much trouble, irritating the Celestial forces, whence arise plagues and pestilence. When we pray God for light—not by words but deeds—He will again turn His face towards us, and, putting an end to our misery and unreason, will restore to us the Light of Nature that it may shine in our understandings as the Sun in the Heavens, without which the Stars give no light.

For our human light, *i.e.*, reason, is by itself dark, and is illumed by this Sun, not by means of ink and paper, but by inspiration. By this Divine Sun alone can the Magical Art be explained.

When man by experience had learnt that, as God out of water had made the Great World, *i.e.*, heaven and earth. with all that therein is, and out of the Great World had made man in His own image, He found that in the small world, *i.e.*, in man, Heaven and Earth and all things contained in the Great World had their counterparts. He also found that all bodies contained three palpable and visible substances: (1) Water; (2) Salt; (3) Sulphur. These three things comprise everything created by God—neither more nor less.

When man learnt how, out of water, through corruption and generation, these three substances are born, he had not yet found his Creator, whose Spirit brooded over the waters, as the Scriptures say. He therefore takes the three bodies, narrowly examines one after the other, reflects that God is a Spirit, invisible to human eyes, and that—since He has created all things—He must be a Living Power. Therefore man takes water, regards it, finds therein nothing but the four elements. Then again taking Sulphur, he finds also nothing therein but the four elements, that is, nothing stable. Lastly he takes Salt—sees there is something more therein than in water and sulphur, yea, he finds two things: (1) A water not different from the former; (2) A Sulphur differing from the former, *i.e.*, a Sulphur which burns not. The third thing he found not, for it vanished from before his eyes. What should he do? It was gone. Where should he find it? He regarded the water, the sulphur, two fine, pure, white substances; but the third. which had lain among them and joined the two together, was departed, and it was the same he had been seeking.

Hence he became very sad, crying day and night unto the Lord, until he found what he sought. But who shall describe how it was found? Or what ears may listen to so great a mystery? Verily, in this is contained the Wisdom of all Celestial and Terrestrial things! Here is the same mystery as when, in the latter times, the Word was made Flesh, the chosen partakers of which see Heaven open with St. Stephen, and the Son of Man sitting at God's right hand. And—with St. Paul—they ascend into the Third Heaven. Hence it is permitted to none to reveal it. Through this mystery the Magi have known the Trinity, and the Incarnation of the Word, and have written concerning the same many centuries before the birth of Christ. But woe to the man who shall reveal this secret in any other way than it has already been revealed! Hence I am to be excused for being silent concerning this Arcanum, which God reserves for His beloved, and will in His mercy reveal to those honestly striving for the same.

To speak farther in respect of the

third substance, wherein is the salt that is water and earth—and of the Spirit of the Lord brooding over the waters: when the Almighty had thus enlightened Man, shewing him how God gives Himself into our hands and dwells in us—in short, with Heaven and Earth, is in us and about us—He thus shewed him the great love that He bears to Man, that He is always near to him, delivering him from all evil so soon as Man knows His name—*i.e.*, knows where He is and when and where to find Him. Yet is this not in phantasies and thoughts, not in books, but in Heaven—*i.e.*, in Man himself—not in subtle speculations, but with diligence and labour, in the sweat of his brow. Who can measure the joy of Man when he had obtained a knowledge of his Creator, or comprehend the Grace communicated to him by God through such knowledge; for what could he desire on earth that would thereby not be given him? He had for his bodily, human needs Medicine to restore his health. He had his daily bread, peace upon earth, and, after this life, Eternity. That was the fruit of the field he tilled in the sweat of his brow, that the reward of his Lord; for he served Him not by words, but deeds; not by speculation, but by his handiwork in the sweat of his brow. And as the service was, so the reward—*i.e.*, in works, not spiritually and phantastically—as happens now-a-days to many who, in armchairs and warm rooms, comfortably imagine remedies against diseases until they produce a phantastical recipe for their patient, which, however, does not help the sufferer. Thus does the Master of Lies recompense his followers. But the Master of Truth hates such chatter, and adorns His children with miracles. It is a great scandal that a sick man, created in God's image, should seek that help from the creature which the Creator alone can give. But, as we know Him, so does He help us.

Therefore Man was right to rejoice at having found his Saviour and Creator, who supplied all his wants. Therefore

Man also helped his neighbour in his need, fed him when hungry, comforted him when dying. Therefore also he found ways and means to preserve this Divine knowledge for his descendants, and wrote three books:

In the First he treated of God the Father, Son, and Holy Ghost.

In the Second of Heaven and its Stars.

In the Third of the powers of the things growing out of the earth.

These three subjects being:

(1) Theology, (2) Astronomy, (3) Medicine.

By means of Theology he teaches and describes the *Middle Substance* among the other three—*i.e.*, the Spirit of the Lord.

Astronomy treats of the *Water*, over which the Spirit of the Lord brooded.

By means of Medicine he describes the third substance—*i.e.*, *Earth*—which, through the Spirit of the Lord, was joined to, and made one thing with, water. Thus also Astronomy and Medicine, through Theology, are united into one—*i.e.*, are three in one substance.

In order to communicate his knowledge aright he was obliged to arrange his subject into the above triadic divisions. For had he comprised everything in one Science, great confusion would have resulted.

These three books were revealed by him to his children and kinsmen.

Thus did the knowledge of Theology, Astronomy, and Medicine grow. Each one studied what he was fit for according to his capacity. Now, these people were called Magi—*i.e.*, wise men—who were of more account than others; hence, also, were they kings, princes, priests, and lords. These did great wonders among the people, curing the sick, restoring sight to the blind, cleansing the lepers, healing the dropsical, giving alms to the poor.

The other people, who were not Magi, considered them more as gods than as men.

Thus came Theology, Astronomy, and Medicine into the world.

The Spirit, by inspiration of which these Magi wrote, remained with them alone; the books got amongst the people. When now the common man saw the wonders described by the Magi, he—having possession of these books—thought himself already a Magus, and wished to accomplish the works of one, especially in Medicine. But when it came to acts he found difficulties, and his ignorance of the hidden sense caused him to interpret these books according to his own imagination.

For instance, when he read: "Scammony purges bile," or "Wallwort (dwarf-alder) cures dropsy," etc.— he sought until he found some herb "rumbling through the belly," and, jumping to the conclusion that bile was thereby purged, the same herb was in future his Scammony of the Magi. Again, on discovering a herb of some little use in dropsy, he set it down as the wall-wort of the Magi. A herb of some effect in fevers was the Camomile of the Magi, and so on.

Thus were Commentaries on Medicine written, and there arose a Sect calling themselves physicians, multiplying as weeds are wont to do. When now the Magi died out (perhaps God would have it so), true Medicine also died out with them; and after their death there remained this Sect, who ignorantly arrogated to themselves a knowledge of the Magical Books. They, however, were not kings, princes, priests, or lords—they were beggars, who by their chatter sought money and goods and honours with the people. The greatest chatterer was accounted the best physician.

These also wrote many books concerning herbs and diseases. In the course of time the true volumes of Wisdom got lost—what could be done with them? They were too hard to understand! Thus it happens that in our own time we have none of them.

In a similar way was Theology

treated. Ignorant men intruded themselves into this Science also. Possessing the written words, they imagined they knew God, and farther study was unnecessary! So these were Mouth-and-Belly-Theologians, making much noise among the people. But they healed no sick, restored not the lame and blind. It was not their province, but that of the physicians, to wit!

The same thing happened in Astronomy. They beheld the Moon, Sun, and Stars rise and set, and, having made these elementary observations, straightway considered themselves Astronomers. Imagining many spheres and circles, they wrote many imposing volumes about them. Who could contradict or expose them? The Magi were dead, and the world was filled with lies; and so it remains to this day. How could God punish the world more severely than by permitting these false teachers, who knew not the true origin of the three Faculties?

Thus came Theologians into the

world. They have received their spiritual understanding, not from the Magi, not from the Light of Nature— by the light of which we may know Him and His creatures, as the Magi found Him – but from Theology, in which they have darkened the secrets of God to the utmost, so that the knowledge of God, *i.e.*, the treasure of the whole world, might remain with them alone, when it should be the possession of all those to whom God reveals Himself. Why then should he not also reveal Himself unto us? Are we not men as well as they? I reply, there is an impediment in our sloth. It is much easier to sit in church for an hour, listening to another, or at home to read one book after another, than with all resources of body, mind, and estate, in the sweat of our brow, to seek diligently after the Living Spirit of God—breathed by Him into the lump of earth when Adam was created—which opens our eyes, revealing the secrets of Holy Writ, of Peter, of Paul, and of the Apostles. Thus may we become theologians, useful to the world, and able to help our neighbour in his need. Thus also may we receive from the Spirit of the Lord in us health and peace, may know the Son of Man, and how His Flesh transmutes our flesh into His Flesh and Life Eternal. But, say the Theologians, we have read the Scriptures and theological works, we possess the plain truth—what more would you have? And they testify as to their doctrine, and as to whom has made theologians of them, by stirring up one country against another, and by causing misery in the world.

They have found a sign in the Church, *viz.*, that of water. Had they sufficient understanding to know the meaning of this symbol, they would also know what their Theology was worth. But to this hour not one of them understands the mystery, which, according to their opinion, is a Jewish or Heathen thing. Thus, also, have they rejected many Magical and Apostolical observances. Had they inquired into the causes of these observances, they would have discovered them to be Magical books, which give us as deep an, or even a deeper, insight into God's Mysterises than written books. Such Magical books have been in the Church from the beginning. They are not hidden away in boxes, but are open to everyone; and are to be found among Jews and Heathens, Turks and Tartars, but chiefly among Christians. They are there for rich and poor, learned and unlearned, crying out every day, and teaching us the way to truth. But who hears them? Have we not ears to hear their cries? Priests, monks, and nuns go about amongst us, and know themselves not what they do. The Ark of the Testament is covered; they know about as much as you. But never heed them; they speak but as they have been taught. Look rather up on High, reflect why we are here, consider what He knows Who has willed that we also should have knowledge, and you will receive Salvation from God. Inquire not after them what they do; they must do this for their daily bread. Let their chatter be. You have Moses and the Prophets, Christ and the Apostles; hear what they say. They speak not with the mouth alone, but with hands and feet, with fire and water, with silver and gold, with salt, with silk, with velvet, with stone, with black, with white, with red, with yellow, with wax, and with oil, etc. Hear not alone what the mouth says, hear what the water says, what the salt says. They also speak, but another tongue. Learn this, and then Scribes and Pharisees will not be able to lead you astray, nor cause strife among you; yea, you will have peace in your conscience towards God and your neighbour.

But if you hearken not to what we say, holding their works and books as sacred, you will be led away from one Sect to another, and suffer damage and shame in your bodies, wife, children, land, and servants. Your enemies will consume you, and thus shall be your reward for the wisdom falsely imagined.

by you from the letter of our books. Therefore, hearken to our words. Learn to read these books, in which are no allegories, no metaphors, no parables, but the naked Truth. We are able to expound the Old and the New Testaments, not this or that peasant who has just come from the plough. Thus is it written in the Book of Ecclesiastes: "Happy is he who knoweth her voice" (the voice of Truth).

Medicine has also its Revelations, which have brought it to honour.

(1) The Books written by the Magi themselves. (2) The Signs which they, for our benefit, have chosen and appointed. For, when in the beginning the three Faculties were described, to each were signs given by which it might be interpreted, and for this cause: that if the Books were lost—as afterwards happened to the one Faculty of Medicine—something should remain by which Truth might be learnt. Hence to each Faculty certain imperishable signs are appointed.

Of all the theological books, the two Testaments alone remain to us. There are also theological signs (that we might have other books in case the written ones were lost), such as: the Mass, Hymns, etc., of which we have sufficiently treated above. The Medicinal books, written by the Magi, are all lost. We have the signs alone. These are: all herbs and trees upon the earth. These signs are now our books, written by God Almighty alone, Who, in His boundless mercy, has communicated to us such books; not that these books are our health—just as in Theology the Church Ordinances are not our salvation—but that from them we should find health and salvation, by a right knowledge of the God Who ordained them. Many self-styled clever people, seeing that masses, singing, and organ-playing, wax and oil, and salt cannot save us, have rejected them. Why do not the doctors of Medicine do likewise? They see that Elder, Saxifrage, etc., do not cure Stone and Podagra, as the books relate. Why do they not forbid the earth to bear such fruits, since they do not what is written concerning them? It is not thus. God has created the earth and adorned it with its fruit, just as God's Houses have, by God's learned people, been adorned, which ornaments also will doubtless remain. The earth will keep its flowers, although Podagra be not cured thereby. Thus, the herbs and flowers are not the medicines, but only signs to point Medicine out to us, just as the Sacraments point God out to us, not that they are God, but appointed by God's Word, even as the herbs in the fields are created by the same. It is written: " Chelidonia (Swallow-wort) cures jaundice." A book-learned doctor taking Chelidonia fails to cure jaundice therewith. Whose fault is it? That of God's creatures, or of the Magi, or of the doctor disappointed of his fee? Verily, although with Chelidonia jaundice cannot be cured, yet its praise will doubtless remain in the books of Medicine. Not in those studied by armchair students, but in the books written by God Himself. These are the earth, with its herbs and flowers, given us by the Magi to teach us the Science of Medicine when their books were lost (which has now occurred). Thus Chelidonia indicates to us the remedy for jaundice; not that it is the remedy, but a Medicinal Sign. Thus also with other plants. But we wish to hear nothing of Magic, writing stately volumes, according to our thoughts, concerning herbs—taking the Sign for the thing designated, and filling books with the virtues of this or that plant. We give large sums for such books, go to Bologna, Padua, hear much chatter about Medicine, but see no leper cleansed, no dropsy or podagra healed. We spend much money, and at last get a red (doctor's) hat for our pains. But in time of need, when a cure is to be effected, all such chatter is not worth an empty nut.

What shall we say concerning the third Book of Wisdom, Astronomy?

We have its Magical Books, although cruelly mutilated and sophisticated. We have also its signs, viz. :—Sun, Moon, Stars, and the whole Firmament. But this Faculty has fared like the other two. We confound the thing designated with the sign, *i.e.*, the Firmament and Magical Books—not having yet learnt that a nut has both shell and kernel. But the kernel is not the shell, nor the shell the kernel. The Sun, Moon, and Firmament are the Signs which every peasant can see, but the thing designated is understood alone by the divinely taught man. He knows that there is another and different Heaven, Firmament, Sun, and Moon from that which thy red hat can teach us. He knows that the Theology of the old world foreshadows its Messiah. He knows that God has created two worlds, two Heavens, two earths. He knows also that one world has its Theology, Astronomy, and Medicine, and that the Astronomy of the Greater World indicates the Sun and Moon of the Lesser (*i.e.*, man); so also the Medicine of the Greater indicates that of the Lesser.

Thus the outward world represents and explains the inner one. The former is the sign, the latter the thing indicated. Therefore, also, church ceremonies, etc., are not my salvation, but **God dwelling in me through Jesus Christ and Faith.**

The Sun and Moon I see above me influence me neither for good nor bad, but the Sun and Moon and Planets, with which God's Providence has adorned the Heaven in me, which also is the seat of the Almighty, these have the power to rule and reform me according to their course ordained by God.

Wall-wort and Elder growing in the earth of the Great World cannot expel dropsy, nor the Strawberry plant cure leprosy. But the Wall-wort, Elder, etc., growing in the earth in our little world, they do so. But of this earth with its fruits, of this Heaven and Stars, of God and our salvation, one hears naught at Paris, Bologna, Louvain, Wittemberg, etc. They have never tasted the sweetness of this Kernel, but have spread the bitterness of the husks over the whole world. I therefore conclude, having described:

I. How the Spirit of the Lord brooded over the waters before God created Heaven and Earth.

II. How, out of the same water, God created the Greater World, *i.e.*, Heaven and Earth.

III. How, out of the Greater World, He created the Small World (*i.e.*, man), a small Heaven and small Earth.

IV. How God has set His Seat in Heaven, that is, in the Heaven in man.

V. I have shewn that man, with his human understanding, could not comprehend God; but having sought his Saviour in the sweat of his brow, he at last found Him. That from Him he learnt all Nature's secrets, writing an account of the same in books, and explaining the same to his children. That, by the dying out of his race, the common man had obtained possession of these books, and, in his ignorance, had retained the husks instead of the kernel. That through this many Sects had arisen, which continue to this day, and doubtless will remain to the world's end.

Therefore, those who would be professors of Theology, Astronomy, or Medicine, should learn Magic before going to Bologna or Paris; that is, the Art of finding the Lord in His creatures, the Fiat by which the world was created; that is, the Seed of Heaven and earth, the Breath of God, which, breathed into a dead lump of Earth, made of the same a living man.

This Art knows all secrets in Heaven and Earth, and can teach us to know God, to understand the Incarnation of Jesus Christ and all things in Theology. It shews us our Sun and Moon, Planets and Stars, as they rule in us, making peace and friendship with one another, according to the teaching of Astronomy. The same also reveals to us the true Hermodactylus, cure for Podagra; the true Ebulus, healing dropsy; the Coloquint, expelling ague; the Crocus, strengthening the heart, etc. This Art is our Theologian, Astronomer, and Medicus, a right and true schoolmaster, crowning his disciples with miracles, standing by them in all needs; yea, leading them out of this life to Him out of Whose mouth it came into the world.

Did but Theologians learn the interpretation of the Scriptures from this Art, and not from themselves, there would be no Sects, but all would be united, even as the Apostles were united when taught by the Holy Spirit sent to them by Christ. Even the Apostles could not fully understand Christ—although he was daily with them, personally teaching them, etc.—before the coming of the Holy Ghost. We also cannot understand the Sacred Scriptures except by interpretation of the Holy Spirit.

Let us not dare to expound these Scriptures, unless Christ eats and drinks with us, that is, is personally with us as one man with another. Although we have books, let us not boast that we understand them. Why did not the Disciples understand? They heard the Doctrine of Christ from His own mouth, which, verily, is much more than reading it in books; had they understood the same, what need had they of the Holy Spirit? But it was impossible to them, and much more so to us. The Spirit of the Lord must first open our eyes and enlighten our understanding; then shall we know the One God, and have one Religion like the Apostles. What man learned in the Scriptures has ever discovered from the literal words that there are Arts by which Man may be made a partaker of that Spirit which moved upon the face of the waters and was breathed into Adam?

We know that St. Paul—when he, as a Pharisee, together with many other learned Jews, persecuted the Christians—could in no wise be persuaded that Christ was made Man. But, having come to a knowledge of God through the Holy Spirit, he believed the same. We also know that St. Paul communicated this mystery to the highly learned Areopagite Dionysius, who believed, and became a Christian and an Apostle of the Gauls.

It might be objected that, since the same concerns our Souls' Salvation, this mystery should have been plainly described. It is not necessary to put the food into the raven's mouth. Let him fly to it! Thus, also, was it not necessary to reveal this mystery otherwise than through the three Faculties. But why this was not necessary I shall tell you as little as those have told who have gone before me. I may have erred in communicating to you as much as I have. It has been done for your sake, because I see you are a Christian man, earnestly seeking the Truth. For what I have revealed to you is more than I would to others. Accept this as an indication of my mind towards you—for you have not deserted my brother in his need. Therefore have I thought it my duty to communicate to you, before all others, what God (without any boast of mine) has given me. Also, do not think I have written for anyone's hurt; above all, not to injure the learned, to whom I would do all the good in my power. I have written for the simple Truth's sake, and for your benefit, and therefore beg of you to accept it with a single mind. Most cordially commending myself, etc., etc.

AN EXPLANATION OF THE NATURAL PHILOSOPHER'S TINCTURE, OF THEOPHRASTUS PARACELSUS.

By ALEXANDER VON SUCHTEN,
Doctor of Philosophy and of Medicine.

THE ancient teacher Hieronymus says that it was formerly ordained among the Jews that no one under the age of thirty years might read the first Chapter of Genesis. Be this true or not, it is certainly not the custom among the Jews at the present time. Yet it is undeniable that man by a right contemplation and understanding of this Chapter, may gain a knowledge of many Arcana and secrets of creation. Not to mention other things, this Chapter is especially suitable to our Chemical Art. Indeed, of all books concerning the Theory and Practice of the Philosopher's Stone, I know not of one which, from beginning to end, could more plainly and graphically describe our Art, than the Almighty Himself has done in that whole process of His great Creation. Since, however, Theophrastus diligently, and above all others, in his book, *Tinctura Physicorum*, followed in the way prescribed by God, and in the aforesaid book has sufficiently described both the matter and Practice—or handiwork—both of the Ancient Philosophers as well as of his own new corrected opinion, I will in this place substitute no other practice, but simply give a short Guide for the better understanding of his book in order that beginners in this Art (I write not for the learned) may, by diligent study, and God's Grace, attain to, not alone an understanding of the above Theoretical Fundament, but also the necessary manual skill in this Art from beginning to end.

Theophrastus, in describing this our philosophical work and creation (which is none other than a small world, since in it appear the participation and similitude of all things), follows the same method as Moses in describing the creation of the Great World. For, before Moses treats of the matter, he enumerates the three principles which indistinctly lay therein, but which, by God, were distinctly developed from the same. So also does Theophrastus, for, before giving the matter of his work, he indicates that, although it is one thing, three things lie hidden in it. These must, by fire or water, be extracted, and again be united into one being and substance, according to Christ's saying: "He who knoweth not to extract many things from one thing, the same knoweth also not to make one out of many." Now, Theophrastus says: "The matter of the Tincture is One Thing that, by fire, has been extracted out of three." This is to be understood as the general consensus of all philosophers. What

Theophrastus here affirms, Geber also substantiates. There is one Stone, one Medicine, to "which we neither add, nor take from it, anything."

Bernhardus says: "There is a single root from which the two Mercurial Substances and our whole work are extracted or made."

Morienus says: "The first and principal substance of this thing is one, and out of it is one thing."

Agadmon, in the *Turba*, testifies also: "Therefore dismiss all plurality, for Nature is content with one thing," etc.

Hermes, a father of all philosophers, also says in his *Tabula*: "Even as all things have been born from one, by the mediation of One, so also all things have been born from this one thing, by adaptation."

Hercules especially agrees with Theophrastus, saying: "This Magisterium proceeds from one root, which afterwards is expanded into several things, returning again to one." (See Pandor., fol. 8,706.)

From all of which the Truth and foundation of this Art is apparent, for Truth is where there appears no contradiction.

Therefore also can false Alchemists be easily detected in this one point alone.

And since God Almighty Himself has created the whole great World, all Celestial, Animal, Vegetable, and Mineral Natures from one single thing and primeval root, how should Man be wiser than God, and for this work—which, not less than the Great Outer World, contains within itself the seed and qualities of all creatures—use more than one thing.

For the said Art—according to the testimony of Ferrariensis, Chap. 22—should imitate Nature. The matter of Art will be the matter of Nature, and, since the matter of Nature is unique, viz., the origin and matter of metals—therefore, also, the matter of Art will be unique. The Book of Genesis relates that this primary matter was of a moist nature, or water, for, when diligently reading the text, although the three principles are first enumerated, viz., Heaven, Earth, and the Spirit of God; yet there soon follows the matter out of which God created Heaven, viz., water, which God took and divided into two parts or pieces, as you will hear. Hermes, or Mercurius Trismegistus, although an Egyptian priest, without enlightenment from God, may yet have derived great wisdom from writings perhaps left behind by Moses after the Exodus. Hermes names not alone the matter from which all elements are drawn, a moist nature, but alludes pointedly to the division. (Pymander, Chap. I.) "This Word (Spirit), moving over humid nature, cherished it. But ardent and light fire straightway flew out from the bowels of humid nature; also light air, obedient to the Spirit, took the middle place between fire and water. Earth and water lay mixed with each other, so that the face of the earth might nowhere appear, being drowned by the waters. Then these two were separated by the Spiritual Word."

Also Plato: "Water is the principle of the universe. For, from water are all things produced, and into water all reduced." Hermes calls water the principle of all things. Theophrastus is herein of the same opinion, except that he does not expressly call matter water or moist nature. But he says it is composed of three substances, calling them here an Eagle, a Lion, and a Golden Glitter.

In *Liber Metamorphoseos* he terms them: Mercury, Salt, and Sulphur. That is just the opinion of Hermes and other philosophers, speaking of Spirit, Body, and Soul. (See *Key of Chemical Philosophy*, by Dornæus, fol. 411.) How, now, these three can, by the artist, by means of Vulcan's art, be extracted and freed from their prison, and again be united, will follow later. Remember, for the present, that he calls the one thing, from which shall be born the great and also the little world, a Red

Lion. Had he desired to indicate it more plainly, he would have called it a moist nature, or water. He does this to prevent the unworthy from sharing this secret with the worthy. Other philosophers have exercised the same caution. For it is written "This stone is hidden both from men and from demons." But it is called a Lion on account of its great strength and power. For as a lion is the strongest and fleetest animal, mastering the other animals, and therefore compared to a king of beasts—so also, amongst things created, there will not easily be found a fleeter, stronger, more penetrating thing, subjugating, occupying, overcoming, and ruling, without exception, man and others.

Hermes confirms such swift strength, saying: "This matter is the strongest strength of all strength." This is also experienced by those who know this Lion, and by proper preparation have been instructed how to use it upon other creatures. Then one sees after what manner this thing occupies, conquers, destroys, kills all things, even changing them from one form into another, nothing being exempt from its rule or unterrified by its roars. Hence by philosophers it is named the "Animated Thing." Hermes says: "Behold, it conquers every subtle, and penetrates every solid, substance!" For this reason Dionysius Zacharias calls it a Governor, and Bernhardus a King. For there is nothing can bear so much rain, wind, work, heat, or cold, while it can be conquered or killed by nothing—except it be by water—as those know who have had such monsters in their keeping. Therefore it may be rightly named a strong Lion, by reason of the temperate conjunction of the Elements. For those Elements are separated and purified, and alternately married in a suitable manner, there being generated from them a Tempered Substance, which the Violence of Fire cannot separate, nor earth's corruption vitiate, nor the muddiness of Water condemn, nor the contact of Air cloud. In order that one should not imagine such

Lion to be a strange, rare thing, he, Bernhardus, says: "This Lion is named by many but known by few." And it is true that it is at the present day carried about by all sorts of men in their mouths, although few, yea, only those whose eyes God has opened to Nature's virtues and powers, can recognise and use it. Yet in its substance, nature, and matter it is so common, often-used a thing that Bernhardus says: "The whole world have it before their eyes." Morienus asserts it to be so universal that Man could not live without it. Verily, "I declare to thee," quoth he to King Calid, "that this Thing by Divine Will has been greatly used in Creation, and nothing made by God can exist without it." Every person knows this thing, and whoso knows it not, he knows nothing else. I should like to see a child of seven or eight who is not acquainted therewith, and is without a hearty appetite and desire for it immediately he beholds it. This inclination proceeds from man's inner spirit, which well knows that all power to preserve health and long life are hidden in this one thing alone. And, in order that this substance be revealed and made known, he gives you another hint and sign whereby you yourself may recognise it, saying: "Such matter is the Greatest Pearl and Noblest Treasure upon Earth according to God's Revelation and man's desire." These words are literally copied from the Lesser Rosary, which says: "For God has under Heaven created no more precious thing, except the rational mind." Examine one after the other all creatures, you will find among them all no more precious, better, more lovely, or nobler creature created by God. An intelligent man can easily find bottom here by diligently observing the above explanations, together with the Sympathy and Disposition (Diathesis) of God's creation with respect to man's natural life. I will let the above instances and the guiding of Theophrastus suffice, and now refer you to our Author's little Book,

De Viribus Spiritualium, where he speaks of the Spirit of Life. There you will find that the *Spiritus Vitæ*, or man's life, is itself a celestial, invisible vapour; it is the temperament between the Elements, and is included in the Stars and all Heaven's influences as far as the firmament stretches. Cornelius Agrippa, in Book I., "Concerning Occult Philosophy," and the Spirit of the World, teaches how and by what means such Spirit is attracted from the Stars into nether corporeal bodies by their Magnetic Force.

Richard, the Englishman, also teaches the same fully in his *Corrector. Alchy.*, part v., chap. 8 and 9: "When you now have found which most abundantly partakes of this Influx and Spirit of Life from other, the same you may use for your work, and apply it by right means and preparation, using its Spirit for the strengthening, preservation, and augmentation of your own spirit. This is more than enough concerning the matter."

Now he comes to the preparation, and to the before-mentioned three principles, saying: "That this Lion, by Nature's aid and the artist's art, may be transmuted into the White Eagle, and thus, out of one, two are made."

Here the Author has wished to signify that, in this Art, man must follow the rule left him by God, the First Chemist. For, God having created all Creatures and Elements out of one thing, viz., Water, it follows that He began by making two things out of the original one thing. The first He has taken up on high, making of it a heavenly water; the other was gathered together below, and by coagulation became Earth. St. Peter, II., chap. 3, briefly mentions these three principles: "By the word of God the Heavens were of old, and the Earth standing out of the Water and in the Water." Esdras, Book 4, the last chapter, says: "For God hangs the Earth over the Waters by His Word."

Thus also in this work the Artist must divide his process into two parts:

(1) By distillation conduct one part on high, making of it a clear, heavenly Spiritual Water, here called a White Eagle. For, as no bird is so keen-sighted, or soars so high as the eagle, so also we know of no water so volatile, so penetrating as this, for it ascends to the Heavens; and, as the Lion's father and son, penetrates his bone and marrow, as we shall presently shew. Our Eagle is the true key to human renovation, and the bath of new Birth and Rejuvenation, as saith the Psalmist: " Like the Eagle shalt thou renew thy youth." It is a white transparent Water of heavenly colour, according to Alanus and Bernhardus, and hence is by many called Heaven (Cœlum) by reason of its lofty qualities.

This Eagle is the first part of the water which ascends on high, the Ascendens of Hermes mentioned in his *Tabula*.

Esdras, Book 4, calls it: " The

Spirit of the Firmament." Other philosophers term it "Water, Spirit, or Soul of the World, the middle Nature which is a quasi-body and quasi-not-soul, and quasi-soul and quasi-not-body. It is the ligament and vinculum of all Elements—also, the one universal, generative Nature, dispersed through all the parts of the world."

And, since it has its centre in the Supreme Circle (as being very light), whence also it came in the First Universal Generation of things, so when freed it ascends towards Heaven to its Centre. Above it has been called *Humor Lunæ*, or the "Humid Radical of all Creatures."

Compare Aurelius Augurellus, Book 1, "To the Lion," 10.

For this *(Anima Mundi)* is diffused everywhere,

And everywhere is active;

In the winds of heaven, in the earth, and the bosom of the wide waters.

They enclose the Soul, by which all things of earth do live. Thence the world itself derives its life. But, since the Soul is trammelled by no body, and the world, and all parts thereof, are in material form; therefore, between these two the Spirit is the intermediary, which is neither body, nor Soul, sharing in both these natures.

Therefore in this live and increase Sea, Air, and Fire. This, embracing all things, is always the Bird (Eagle), always the root, ever bringing forth and perpetuating life.

At length, imprisoned in yellow gold, itself seeks the hand of the artificer, who may loose its bonds, and, by its virtue, become powerful.

(2) The other part of the water—or of our Lion—according to the teaching of Moses, became corrupted and dry. That is now the second part of our Art, viz., the investigation of the substance of the Lion, when the aforesaid Eagle has been hatched out of his body, by warmth, as from an egg, and has flown away. To speak plainly concerning it, it is the dry, waste earth, and the cursed

earth in Gen. V. It has its first name of Lion by reason of its aforesaid strength and sharpness. For, as a lion has sharp teeth, biting through and through that which he seizes, so also is this earth so sharp as to be unbearable on the tongue because of its penetrating nature. It cannot be touched without offence to the tongue, as saith the philosopher. Elsewhere Theophrastus calls it, "An invisible, consuming fire."

Bernhardus retains its name of King, and says: "Although Fontin, the aforesaid Eagle, is the King's Mother, yet is the King nobler than Fontin." For, although he always retains the name of Lion, yet is he changed from his first nature, is no longer a virgin, but has been fructified by the Spirit brooding over the water — his original first substance—and has borne a heavenly, spiritual fruit, viz., the aforesaid Eagle. Hence these verses:

A virgin, not one day old,
By Nature's decree espoused a man,

And, before she had reached the age of one year,
To this man a child she bore,
Yet she died before she was born.

And in The Song of Solomon, Chap. VIII., "I raised thee up under the apple-tree, there thy mother brought thee forth: there she brought thee forth that bare thee."

Hermes calls the inferior substance gross or descending. For, being heavy, it has, and seeks, its centre in the lowest circle, as it were, subject to the superior heaven and its influx, or the Soul of Middle Nature, or Mundane Spirit. Above it has been called by its right name of "Solar and Natural Heat" of all corporal and natural things.

Now, as to the third principle, viz., the Spirit brooding, &c. It is, according to Theophrastus the Glitter of Gold. For this Earth is but the real fine Gold, left imperfect by Nature, to be perfected by Art, as Ferrariensis says (Chap. 64): "The terrestrial parts are nothing else than the occult gold of philosophers."

Other sages define it as "The Soul of the World, whose colour is golden." Now, since in the first Universal Creation, the third principle, the Spirit of God, has never been separated from the other two, but the two have remained in one as the Spirit above, and in the water, so also is it in our microcosmic, particularistic, and philosophical Creation. We cannot obtain this third principle, this golden glitter, this beautiful gold-red colour, separate by itself. "It shines not to the Spagyrus," saith Theophrastus, *i.e.*, it conceals itself and is lost when one is made into two. What, then, becomes of it? According to Gen., chap. 1., and the opinion of philosophers, it remains with the aforesaid water, and since that water ascends towards heaven, this Golden Glitter must accompany it in its centre. Theophrastus, however, considers that it remains with the earth, perhaps on account of the Old Testament saying that the Soul is in the Blood, wherefore the Israelites were forbidden to eat it.

Now, it should be noted this Golden Glitter, as the third principle, is often called the Soul, and cannot be produced other than as a red, thick, stagnant blood, —sometimes called the Lion's blood by our author,—and Theophrastus ascribes it to that body which, in the first distillation, goes not over out of the retort (crucible). For herein, say Alchemists, is the whole art, that the gold go out of the retort. And this is true did they but understand the Gold and its Glitter aright. How the glittering spiritual Soul of this third principle—when duly extracted from the Lion's body—hovers above the water, and there yet remain two in one, you will hear afterwards. For the soul cannot exist, out of its centre, as an impalpable, invisible entity without a body. "For a spirit is neither visible nor palpable, except it hath assumed a body from some Element. Hence this spirit—by reason of its noble nature— receives a Body in the highest and noblest Sphere of the Elements, viz., in the Igneous Sphere. Yet, in the fire, this spirit loses not its special nature, neither is it Fire, nor of an igneous nature; although it dwells in Fire, and by many is called Fire of Nature."

Aurelius Augurellus hath these words in his second book: "But another elicits these various hidden parts from pure Blood, and has ordained the Elements to lead them forth;

"That thus these occult spirits might perchance be seen or touched with the hands, or enclosed in a vessel.

"For otherwise they would straightway penetrate the vessel, although imprisoned in hard adamant.

"By violence can no Spirit be forced to remain in any part of the Vast Orb, so greatly does it rejoice to dwell quietly in its own habitation."

Such external Body is the Lion, or dry earth, which retains its redness, its outward aspect, its stagnant blood, which has no exit, the body being not yet open— as one sees in those hanged or suffocated, who stifle in their blood—as the "Book of the Trinity" relates in figures.

Raymundus Lullius says briefly, in *Testamentum Novissimum*, thus: "My son, Quicksilver is water distilled from its earth, and similarly earth is Animated Quicksilver, while the Anima (Soul) is Natural Heat which is bound in the primary Essence of the Elements of Animated Mercury."

Now that this jewel has been presented to you through the Faculty of Philosophy, you have a short guide to the teaching of Theophrastus. Having taken the right philosophical matter, you are now to extract from it two things contained therein, viz., the Eagle (Mercury), and then the Body (the Salt), which, as Everlasting Balsam, contains also the third thing, the Spiritual Soul, the Golden Glitter, or true gold seed. These you shall extract according to the counsel given in Ovid by Medea to Old Jason, who would become young again, viz., that he—by Anatomy—should divide his limbs, and, re-uniting them in a warm bath, he would become younger and of great strength.

But that you may apply the theory, and learn the modus operandi whereby from Unity, two things, and from two, three are obtained, Theophrastus comes to the Practice. "It is the mark of a wise man first to know the causes before putting his hand to the task." Theophrastus shews you two ways—one Ancient, the other discovered and used by himself – saying the Ancients had a very long way "before accomplishing the aforesaid separations and achieving their object. In the beginning they, out of a *Simplex*—or also out of a *Substantivum* like God Himself—and also Theophrastus, have made two things, viz., Water and Earth." And he continues to say: "that Artists have to these two Simplices given the name Lili—afterwards using the said Simplices and not one." But know it is indifferent whether you, in the beginning, use one or two things. If our matter is found in one thing, it will equally well be found in two (Nature having already converted the original One into Two). Such simplicity of the subject Ferrariensis describes well, chapter 12: "The first radical Element, whence all the Elements derive their origin, is Humidity, or Water, *i.e.*, liquefaction." Or, according to others, it is the Earth.

Shortly after he says: "For the Beginning of the World there is One Sole Element, which is Primary Matter, from the Division of which, by reason of opposing qualities, were generated the four Elements, which were in it potentially."

Aurelius Augurellus, Book II., says:
"Besides within there is ordained a
   double force,
Which always both acts and suffers,
As a female and male when together—
Even as a chicken grows in the shell,
By the action of the one and the suffering of the other in turn,
And by cherishing heat externally
   applied."

If you begin with one thing you must first make two of it. But, by taking two, such as Earth and Water—

Nature having educed this Binary from one—you are saved the trouble, and have only to generate the third, which, as aforesaid, is always hidden in one of these two. Thus Lion's Blood is the Bride around whom they dance, viz., the natural red Sulphur or Seed of Gold, ordained by God and Nature to bear its like. But, being mixed and bound up too much with earth and superfluities, it cannot perform its office, except it be freed by one of Vulcan's smiths from all bolts and bands of its natural prison. Therefore have both the Ancient Sages and Theophrastus taken great pains to liberate these Captive Souls from their Eternal Darkness by the Descent to Hell of our Heavenly Eagle—according to Isaias: Those in darkness and the shadow of death see a great light. Thus have the Ancients united the two things, and, after a month's putrefaction, extracted the spirit, that is, the water, with gentle fire by distillation. For this water will not stand a great fire, and if vexed with the same it becomes impatient, angry, and wrath to such an extent that it "knocks all of a heap," as Bernhardus says, the residual matter they treated with strong water until the same went over as a dry spirit. Compare Solomon's Song, II. C.: "Who is this that cometh out of the wilderness like pillars of smoke, perfumed with myrrh and frankincense, with all powders of the merchant?"

Now, this dry spirit is the substance or body of the Lion himself, the sharp earth, the old, miserly, jealous man, who breaks not willingly into the treasury, or likes to give up his golden-yellow oil, and only by force will let his palace be plundered. It is called a dry spirit by reason of the quantity of dominating fire therein, which is none other than the true philosophical Sulphur, as Bernhardus relates in the "Book concerning the Transmutation of Metals." But sulphur is none other than the pure action of Air and Fire, heating and digesting, or decocting, Earth and Water proportionally and homogeneously to themselves. Richardus, the Englishman, also says: "Philosophers' Sulphur is a simple, living Fire, vivifying and maturing, and nothing but a hot and dry vapour generated from the purest terrestrial dryness in which Fire rules in every way."

Now, since all the oil or spirit does not go over at once — in order that none of this gold seed or potable gold as the Lion's greatest treasure might remain behind — they moistened the *corpus mortuum* (residuum) with spirits and, after a month's putrefaction, again distilled over as at first, thus obtaining more of the oil. This moistening, putrefying, and distilling they repeated until the earth was wholly dissolved, and had given up its entire treasure, all the gold having distilled over and become a Mercury, *i.e.*, Water, which has its coagulation or its sulphur in its depths, as Geber says: "Our Mercury has in its depths fixed Sulphur, and nothing sinks in it except Gold." Dionysius

Zacharias well describes this process in his "Practice": "After the Governor of the Firetown (oven, furnace) had retreated, his remaining warriors had long fought the enemy with fire, until they escaped the said enemy by retreating over the water and bridges which they had thrown up behind themselves."

That is the same thing that Æneas did with the tree bearing golden branches. As often as he broke a branch off two grew in its place. Those are the lovely golden-yellow drops falling from the beak of the retort into the receiving vessel, one dripping down after the other, until the Lion has lost his whole heart, blood, and strength. For that is the true Lion of Judah, sent by God to deliver His Peoples from their enemies and sins, in pain and torture to shed His Blood for them. The wound in His Side, whence flow two living streams of Blood and Water, shall be a Fount of Purification to all those drinking therefrom. In these shall such water become the spring of a long, healthy life.

Bernhardus goes on to relate that the Ancients—having got so far that nothing further distilled over from the earth – they again purified the water and oil, removing all remaining bonds, until they at length reached the Pure Fount, and the true, beautiful, golden leaves of the Golden Book. Here are our Adam and Eve naked, for their eyes are opened, and they now see themselves, what was good and bad in their own substance. This is the Rectification whereby they cleansed these two of the accidental impurities of the first Distillation (for the unclean Spirits guarding the treasure in the earth love not to leave the same). This is the first process of our Philosophical Birth, the " Returning into the Mother's Womb," whereby the Rule of God is followed, and the first precepts of chemists are fulfilled, viz., the Reduction into Primary Matter, into the Three Natural Principles, *i.e.*, Animated Spirit, Mercury, and Sulphureous Vapour of Earth. Thereby are separated the Elements and the Pure from the Impure, and, finally, the Seeds of Gold are brought from Darkness to Light, which is nothing less than the Generation of Nature in the Generation of Metals, and "The Process with double Smoke" of Paracelsus. But the above method entailed heavy expenses and much time and labour, all of which the Ancient Sages could have avoided, and obtained the Lion's Treasure by a shorter cut, had they enquired into the matter as diligently as Theophrastus.

Now, I wot there is no one who would not wish to know this shorter method; and, that you may not have to complain of Theophrastus, he shews you another short way, admonishing you also to let the above tedious process be, and to take from the Lion nought but his rosy blood, and from the Eagle the white gluten. These two bodies you must coagulate together and bring into one body, as it were male and female seed.

Now, someone might object thus. Dear Theophrastus, that is the old story which I have long ago heard. The Ancients took nothing more than the Lion's blood and water, and coagulated them. Yet you tell me the same is a brief way to obtain the aforesaid two Mercurial Substances, with little labour and in a short time.

Well, that is true so far. Theophrastus is not so clear here as he might be. But you may easily imagine what the mode of preparation must be if you have diligently studied Theophrastus's other books and preparations, and are otherwise experienced in Chemical labours. You will then find that Chemistry, in the preparation of all arcana (secrets), has two methods, viz., Distillation and Extraction. Whatsoever is to be prepared by Chemistry and brought into its Arcanum, its Tincture, or Quintessence (in which is the power and virtue of all creatures), or is to be cleansed from impeding impurities, that must be done by Distillation or Extraction (which is the same as Solution). There is no other means. As Bernhardus says: "The King never goes forth except the Fountain attract him."

Now, having already heard that he rejects the tedious process of much distillation and purification by reason of its expense, etc., you perceive that he must have used the only other means, viz., "Extraction by Solution."

According to Calid, son of Jazichus: "Solution is the Extraction of the Interior of Things to their Superficies, so that the hidden become manifest." Hence his (Theo.'s) meaning is this: When you of one thing have made two —or have taken two things differently constituted by Nature—let the old process alone; take from the Lion his blood only—*i.e.*, cut out his heart with his own sharp spear—or as Bernhard. says: "Slay the King with his own sharp, poisonous Mercurial Water." In plain words: Extract but from the earth its Tincture or Arcanum, and the blood, the sunshine, the dry spirit immediately all distils over. By such extraction or solution more will be done in a few hours than the Ancient Sages could effect in six months. By the above process the whole work may be completed in ten or twelve months, in which time the Ancients could barely achieve the first step—*i.e.*, Reduction into Primary Matter—as all those know whom God has enlightened, and thought worthy to know this Solution and Extraction.

But misunderstand me not! I speak here, not of the second solution of the earth, but of the first solution of the crude body.

How this solution and extraction is effected it behoves not to tell here more plainly—as our author says—not to put the food right into the bad birds' beaks. As the saying is: He who would reach the open sea must first pass through the narrow straits. That is the blessed place of which Esdras writes (Bk. IV., chap. 2): The path to it is narrow, so that but one man can walk on the same. On one side is Fire, on the other Water. He who would inherit or possess these good things must first undergo much trouble and danger until he find the narrow footpath between Fire and Water, and pass over. Now, having revealed this to you indirectly as far as may be, I would refer you to other philosophers. Remember Geber's rule: "That no Solution should be made, except in its own blood, and that calcined things are more soluble than non-calcined. For, by calcination, they are reduced to the nature of Salts and Alums, which alone are soluble." If you are a true searcher after knowledge, the above will tell you more than too much.

Compare Aurelius Augurell., Book 3: " First, taking thin plates and filings of pure gold,

" Thou shalt crush and pound them into the form of fine powder, or river sand, with frequent blows:

" Until, at length, they become liquid, dissolved by putrid humour from within themselves.

" It will be well here sometimes to pour in large quantities of liquor of their own seed, but by no chance anything foreign."

This is also the aforesaid short process of Theophrastus, whereby you, in a short time, and with little trouble and expense, may find the two said things (of which one is the Father, or Sun, or Red Water, and the other the Mother, or Moon, or White Water) which are necessary for the perpetration of the miracle of the One Thing, and for which good counsel you owe Theophrastus many thanks. Thus, by God's help, is effected the first step of this process, which is done by the hand through Sublimation and Purification. By this the fleshly, corporeal Adam is killed, and Body, Soul, and Spirit, by the natural death, are separated from one another.

Second Operation.
CONJUNCTION.

Now follows the second operation, in which are brought about, by rest and without labour, the fixation and stability of those things which are sublimated and purified. This is the Resurrection from the Dead, in which Soul, Body, and Spirit, after Purification, come together again; and—on our philosophical Last Day—will arise as a new glorified body and a new spiritual man without blemish and sin. In this conjunction of Resurrection are comprised the whole spiritual body and the soul, and thus form One — even as water mixed with water—and are not separated in all Eternity. For in them is no diversity, yea, a Unity and Identity of all three substances, Spirit, Soul, and Body.

Even so it is plain concerning the Identity and Unity of the Trinity in God the Father, Son, and Holy Ghost, which in the Deity are One and the Same, with distinction and diversity in substance.

The aforesaid process would have been no use to the Ancients, or to Theophrastus, had they not known how to bring to fruition, in its due season, the seed thus obtained. But, in order successfully to effect this, they had again to learn from Nature, and more especially from God as a Preceptor, in Genesis, chapter ii., for there it is written thus: Although God had caused the earth to bring forth all kinds of grass, herbs, and trees, yet they could produce no fruit or propagate and increase their kind, until God had first let rain again upon the earth, the water first separated and taken up to Heaven by Himself. And daily experience teaches us that the earth, when dry, is barren, and that nothing can grow unless frequently refreshed by rain or dew. Hence God has again united the water—which He, as the first Distiller, took up on high—with the dry earth, the Inferior with the Superior. The Ancients, following this rule, have often united white water with the Red Lion's blood, as with the Earth (for, coagulated, such blood is earth), according to the teaching of Hermes: "It ascends from the earth into heaven, and again descends to earth, and receives the strength of inferior and superior things." And elsewhere: "Red

Sun is father, White Moon is mother; join them together in one life and disposition." Morienus: "Make the Red Smoke hold the White Smoke in a strong embrace and in a strong vessel, without exhalation of spirits."

Theophrastus also means that, when you have obtained the two things by the short method, viz., the rosy blood and the Eagle's white gluten, you shall thereto add nothing foreign. Compare Solomon's Song, chapter i., 7: "Tell me, O thou whom my soul loveth, where thou makest the flock to rest at noon, for why should I be as one that turneth aside by the flocks of thy companions?" Take these two things alone, and of them again produce Unity—of two Mercurial Substances make one—like body and soul. Of two waters make one by coagulation. For Quicksilver, or our Mercury, is not coagulated by the coagulation caused by extrinsic mixture (except for corruption); but the same is, by its intrinsic Sulphur, coagulated to perfection. This is the

Union of Heaven and Earth, the marriage of Adam and Eve, the Conjunction of Sun and Moon, the right Union of the World's Soul and Spirit with the Earth by the Union of their Centres, as Calid says: "Of all experiments there is none equal to that of conjoining two or more things whose centres are diverse, unless it be the conversion of their matter, and the mutation of their substance and properties from their original nature. Therefore, he who shall be able to change Soul into Body and Body into Soul, and to mix with the same subtle spirits, shall attain all things."

Compare Aurel. Augurell., Book III.: "Perchance here thou mayest seek the numbers and the weight of the things required by thee for perfecting this work.

"Remember, therefore, there are of Things Primordial but Three.

"From these take two; and from these again—if thou judge rightly—one more.

"The Triple Thing will then consist of Gold alone.

"The decocted substances will form one homogeneous mass.

"For, joined together, they differ among themselves in nothing.

"Each ingredient fuses its mass with that of the others."

By this influx our earth is made fruitful, producing in due time all kinds of animal, vegetable, and mineral natures. This is the warm bath in the beginning of May of Bernhardus, expressed of old in the following figure of speech: "The Water of the Air between Heaven and Earth is of all things the Life. For, by its moisture and warmth, it is the medium between water and fire. The Heavens opening rained and dewed these Waters upon the Earth, rendering it moist and sweet as honey. Wherefore also the Earth blossoms, bringing forth divers colours and fruits; and, in the midst, there has grown up a great tree, with silver stem, stretching to the ends of the world; on its branches have sat many birds which have all flown away towards the East; and the raven's head has become white." All the above means but the spiritual generation and new birth of our Adam, through Water and the Spirit, for the same, in its former nature and earthly tabernacle, could not enter the Kingdom of Heaven. Our old Adam must first put on again its original pure nature, and thus, born again through spiritual water, and changed into a spiritual man, may, through much tribulation, enter the Promised Land.

COAGULATION AND IMBIBITION.

But how can such things be? asks the learned and wise Nicodemus. Art thou a Master in Israel, taking upon thyself the highest works in Physics, and knowest thou not that? Well, Theophrastus tells it you plainly in chap. iii., viz., that it is done through the Pelican (for this is the grave in which shall rest our deceased Adam until his resurrection), even unto the third and fourth time, until the whole "Lili," both matters, earth, and water, are dry on the ground. The words, "for the third and fourth time," are to be interpreted as indicating the frequent rainfall necessary for fruition.

The ancient philosophers in their "Small World," following Nature's example, have been wont to divide the white water (which they first produced from their matter) into two or more parts. The first portion they quickly coagulated with the Lion's Blood, by circulation in the Pelican, according to the formula: "Nature knows Nature, Nature rejoices Nature, Nature receives Nature, and yet there is but One Nature, One Genus, One Substance, and One Essence." Song of Solomon, chap. iii., 4: "But I found him whom my soul loveth; I held him and would not let him go, until I had brought him into my mother's house, into my mother's chamber." To this coagulated, dry earth they have added the other portion of the water, moistening and drying by heat three or four times, until the earth has again received into itself the whole of its white water, and thus the whole Lili has become a dry body. Thus the ancients augmented the stone for fixation in the very beginning. Bernhardus says: "The King's bath may be repeated. For the more frequently he be bathed in such saline, Mercurial water, or sulphureous baths, the purer and stronger does he become. It is optional to do this three or four times in the beginning with coagulation, or only once. By frequent moistening you will get more fruit, also the further advantage (by augmenting in the beginning) of not having to do so at the finish."

For the highest degree of purification, wash seven times in Jordan, and you will have many cwts. of water as your reward. Compare Solomon's Song, chap. i.: "Draw me, and we will run after thee; the King hath brought me into his chambers: we will be glad and rejoice in thee."

For our multiplication (according to Raymundus) is nought but the reiteration of the process of our primordial creation. So also Bernhardus, in his book "Concerning the Transmutation of Metals": "As in this process nothing extraneous enters into its first composition, so also the same multiplies nothing that is not of its first composition." But since all generations and corruptions in Nature are caused by heat; and, especially since Nature, in the bringing forth of metals and earths, has no other instrument but a steady, gentle heat, therefore, also, all imitators of this art have been obliged to follow Nature. The steady warmth of the sun ripens every fruit, and the warmer the sun (yet not too dry and alternating with due rains), the better do fruits mature and turn out.

Hence the ancient sages have ever matured this our philosophical Seed by the heat of a sun shining steadily upon our earth and water, in which the other two are included, for "the virtue of fire and air cannot become apparent except in earth and water, virtue only acting through matter." And, as the great world's sun in summer gets hotter and hotter, until it has reached its highest ascension in the Zodiac, so also have all artists always augmented their "little Summer" in temperature until the matter, having been duly boiled and simmered, from black (through various changes of colour) became blood-red. We can assist our matter by heat alone. Hermes says: "Fire is the Regimen." And Bernhardus also states: "That no one goes with the King to the bath but the stoker, whose sole duty it is to keep up the heat, and that his work is greatest at the end, since the bath is easily inflammable." Farrianus is of the same opinion: "The whole strength lies in the fire. By this we discern and unravel the four Elements in that gross mass. By this we further join and combine things into one. By this we imitate the Sun, and perfect the imperfect." In such warmth it attains maturity, ordained but never completed by Nature. For (quoth Theophrastus) Nature brings nothing complete to Light, but man, by spagyric preparation, must lead up to that ordained of Nature. Hence it is said: "Where Nature ends, there Art begins." And: "Through God was our Philosophical Stone by Nature created, and to the same there is nothing wanting but purification and perfection."

It also learns to fight with the fire, so that the same—however great—may gain no advantage over it. Compare Farrianus: "It rejoices in its own fire, just as anything, Vegetable, Animal, or Mineral, is better preserved in the place of its generation than elsewhere."

THE FOUNDATION OF ART.

The contents and foundation of this Art consist in dissolving gold and silver by the right means—with water, or drying with fire of the volatile Philosopher's Mercury—until the same be changed into a powder which cannot be again reduced to a solid body. This powder—if it smoke not when laid on the fire—tinges every imperfect body and Mercury with a lasting gold or silver colour. The gold colours not except it be first changed by the white gold, —*i.e*, by their Philosopher's Mercurial Water—into the black substance they call their earth and *caput corvi* (crow's head), giving the same many names, which white gold is further changed into a vapour, and is our "Fortified Spirit."

Question.—Whether in the Antimony of Philosophers or Marcasita the Philosophers' secret is hidden? The white gold is the secret, for out of the antimony of our black earth is extracted the highest arcanum of Philosophers, which is in effect a ruby liquor, sweet, and red as blood.

The Salt of Metals is the Philosopher's Stone. Hence make salt of the metals without corrosives.

"Adam," said God, "in fixed and not fixed, in these two lie hidden all

Secrets: Thou art the Lesser World."

Abel has written, that his father Adam gave names to all things.

Noah praises the oilstone (soapstone?) saying there is no stone possessing greater virtues.

Attain, therefore, in time a spiritual earth, not fleeing from fire: Because, among all elements the earth alone is fixed, and the Art of Alchemy wishes that its Stone be fixed. Hence it is necessary that at the end of the operation all things should return to earth, *i.e.*, fixation. Hermes' dictum is true: Its strength is integral, if poured into the earth. In such coction or digestion divers colours are to be seen, not less than in Great Nature in the Earth.

For when the wet winter is passed, when the sun shines again, and the earth, during winter covered with water and snow, becomes dry, all manner of curious colours are seen, especially three, viz., black, white, and red. Between these appear divers colours, as a yellowish colour after the virginal white or red; but this is not permanent. The other yellow remains longer, yet not so long as the black, white, or red. Crauser says, in the *Turba:* "Know that it is a twofold thing to make white and red; the one thing is solution, the other decoction." The former takes place in winter, when the earth is covered with snow and water, a certain indication of Putrefaction, a sign of commixture and of the changing of one thing into another, and is the colour of death. Solomon's Song: "I am black but comely, O ye daughters of Jerusalem, as the tents of Kedar, as the curtains of Solomon. Look not upon me because I am black, because the sun hath looked upon me!"

The time of its duration is unequal. In the Bible one finds that the waters of the Flood lasted 156 days.

Bernhardus says: "In 130 days the King puts off his blackness, and appears in his white shirt." *Scala Phil.* gives 140 days for such putrefaction. *Vide Pandor.*, fol. 36. After these follow the other perfect colours, as the white of complete coagulation. Thus, putrefaction takes place in humidity, but the end of putrefaction is dryness: and incineration is a gentle induration, the occultation of humour, the fixation of spirit, the collecting of things diverse, the Renovation of Homogeneity, the adaptation to fire of things fleeing therefrom, and is the colour of regeneration and of semicoction. It lasts also a long time—according to Bernhardus almost 82 days—which is a sign of fixation according to the Dictum of Lucas in the *Turba:* "When our Magnesia is white it lets not the spirit go from it." Theophrastus sets no limit of time to such colours, as, in truth, none can be set, for it depends on the matter.

Compare Aurel. Augurell., Book III.: "Yet scarcely will anyone so exactly compute the years,

"As not either to diminish or add to their number:

"For suitable material will sometimes accelerate the process, and unsuitable retard the same.

"Or intense heat will by a little exceed the measure, but water by much.

"And time and place will vary."

The time will vary according as the artist tends his fire diligently or not. For this our work is a true woman's or cook's work. They simmer and boil and roast until the spit is done to a turn; they wash and dry the linen in the sun until it is snow white. Also this white colour is like unto the earth when dry; then the corn soon gets white also, and is not far from maturity, viz., from the third colour, the yellow. As soon as the same appears in the corn it is cut; the winter is past, the rain over, the flowers have appeared, summer is come, and the turtledove is heard in our land. Thus also is the maturing of our matter, when its yellow colour appears. As regards its metallic nature, and the perfection of the same, we must bring that to a higher grade, says Bernhardus, viz., to its red colour, that it thus may communicate to other imperfect metals some of its superabundant perfection. For this redness is the sign of incorruptibility and complete digestion.

Just so Christ became more than perfect in the highest exaltation of His humanity through His rosy blood, in obedience, in fulfilling and satisfying the Law, and in love towards God, in order to communicate to us, His people, of its fulness, through the Holy Spirit, whereby we might become heirs and sharers of His Kingdom. In this our Elias goes up to heaven in a storm and seated in a fiery chariot. Now go forth, ye daughters of Jerusalem, and behold King Solomon crowned by his mother on the day of his marriage and of his heart's joy. Every diligent student will now, without further explanation, be able to find these colours. Consult the philosophers concerning the same: Bernhardus, *Scala Phil.*, etc., etc.

Attention must, during such coction, be paid to the proper order of the colours produced, for with them change the qualities of the active agent, demanding a corresponding mutation in the passive reagent. For, in our solution, the water is first active, the earth then attracting the King, but in coagulation it is passive. This change of mode cannot take place without development of divers colours, which is expressed by philosophers thus: "Heat acting on moisture generates blackness, and, acting on dryness, generates whiteness, in which redness is hidden."

Solomon mentions such coction and colours in his Song, chap. v., 10: "My beloved is white and ruddy, the chiefest among ten thousand. His head is as the most fine gold, his locks are bushy and black as a raven. His eyes are as doves' eyes by rivers of waters, washed with milk and fitly set. His cheeks are as a bed of spices, as sweet flowers: his lips like lilies, dropping sweet-smelling myrrh. His hands are as gold rings, set with the beryl: his belly is as bright ivory, overlaid with sapphires. His legs are as pillars of marble, set upon sockets of fine gold." The ancient Sages have also mentioned the same in parables, as when they saw a mist rise in the distance (possibly the mist that watered the whole earth). They saw also the violence of the sea and of the water-floods upon the face of the earth, that the same stank in the darkness (putrefaction). They also beheld the King of the Earth sink, and heard him cry with a terrible voice: He who delivers me shall live for ever, and rule in my glory on my royal throne, and all things shall be given into his power (*i.e.*, blackness). On the following day they beheld above the King a most beautiful morning star, and the light of day illumining the darkness (*i.e.*, whiteness), the bright sun rising through brilliant clouds of various forms and colours (*i.e.*, yellowness and redness). Then, in fulness of time, the King was crowned with three costly crowns, of iron, of silver, and of pure gold. In his right hand they saw a sceptre with seven glittering stars, and in his left a golden apple, upon which was sitting a white dove, with silvery body and golden wings.

But particularly is the frequent imbibition (moistening) of dry earth with water described and indicated in complete parables—(Philosophers have given this process of imbibition many other names, such as Exaltation, Fermentation, etc., but they are all one, viz., the subtilization of White and Red, and the augmentation of excellence and quantity). They beheld a man, as black as a Moor, stuck fast in a black stagnant bog, to whose assistance came a young woman, beautiful of countenance, and clad in bright apparel. Her back was adorned with glorious white wings and golden feathers, and on her knees she wore fine pearls. On her head she had a crown of pure gold, set with a silver star, around her neck a necklet of gold, set with precious stones, and on her feet golden shoes. From her proceeded the most sweet scent, above all aromas.

She clothes man with a purple robe, inspires him with highest wisdom, and leads him to Heaven. By diligently exercising yourself in suchlike parables, and—at the same time—paying attention to the works of Nature in the great generation, you will not only be able to await a plentiful harvest in due course, but will so increase the store of your philosophical oil, or tincture, as to be short of vessels into which to pour the same; even as the widow of Elisha. Thus shall you be free from debt and feed your house in plenty; for your meal shall not diminish nor your cruse be wanting.

There is nothing said here of the fire whereby this artificial coction takes place. Perhaps it is the everlasting fire, of which many Alchemists boast, the fire used aforetime by the Jews for their burnt offerings, which burnt continually without becoming extinguished, which also was hidden by the Prophet Jeremiah before the first destruction of Jerusalem, and afterwards was discovered by Ezra.

The same is said to have been thick and oily, like oil or honey, as Josephus describes it. If you can and will prepare it, good; if not, refer to the *Turba*, Chrysippus, etc., for they will give you a good account, saying that this fire may be prepared in many ways, always taking care not to let the active principle escape, or, as Bernhardus explains it: Not to let the bath take fire, and flee away like a fugitive eagle, thus causing a dissipation of seed and preventing generation. "For then the Elements will not combine, but will vanish by fire, on account of the strength of the spirit and of the dominating and operating volatile thing; so wilt thou become poor, and lose that which thou hast."

Hence the "triple vase" commonly used by Philosophers, and the "old hollow oak split through the middle," viz., the oaken sphere of Bernhardus, in whose middle is the clear stone, in which stood the bath. All this was done to ward off the too strong rays of the Sun, that our male and female seed might, without hindrance, remain together to the birth: "For the separation of active and passive necessarily prevents generation."

Compare Solomon's Song, chapter ii.: "I charge you, O ye daughters of Jerusalem, that ye wake not my love till he please."

When Theophrastus further speaks of Hungary, Istria, the South, or Cyprus, he gives you to understand in which countries our matter ought to be sought, and he leaves it to you whether you will have two different substances which, as regards their genus, are of one and the same nature. Therefore, seek the one, the Lion, in Hungary; but the Eagle in Istria. But if you rule your work through one thing, thus proceeding from Unity to Duality, and thence to three things, then travel to Cyprus. There you will be refused nothing.

Bernhardus has travelled yet farther, saying that he fetched his man, viz., the chosen jewel, the golden book, from India. Christophorus Parisiensis also went far for the same, and says: "When you now quit the town of Venice, go far to the right until you find a pleasant level country: there is our Mercury." Whether in liquid or coagulated form, it is best to obtain it from the above-named places, by reason of its beautiful red colour. Although found also in Germany and other countries—Theophrastus saying elsewhere that of the perfect Medicine enough is found in Germany—yet the native article is not so good and strong as the foreign. "For the virtue is dispersed, and less united, therefore less strong. For here masculine and feminine are substantively the same, and in the one subject are combined different and contrary virtues, since our Lion is hermaphrodite."

If you use but one thing, make of the same two, but, lastly, of one of these three. Afterwards for these three build a tabernacle, and diligently take heed that the sacred Threefoldness be reduced through Duality to Unity, the Author of all consummate perfection. So from our New Earth and New Heaven (the old Earth and Heaven having been destroyed by fire, together with their works) you will have a New World, the Holy Place, the New Jerusalem, as a bride for the bridegroom, wherein all tears, lamentation, and sorrow shall be no more, whose gates also are adorned with all manner of precious stones and pearls, the streets are of pure gold like unto a beautiful mirror, and the names of the dwellers therein are all written in the Book of Life.

There all things are new, for the former things have passed away; and, as Hermes briefly says: "Thou shalt have the World's Glory and all thy desire."

Finally, as regards the utility of the Medicine thus prepared, the same is sufficiently described in other books. That this Medicine is of great use with respect to the health of the human body may easily be gathered from the aforesaid Medicinal Foundation. For this our philosophical Son, a Son of Sun and Moon, which rule the whole world, as a learned Astronomer has traversed all planetary spheres and the whole firmament in his colours. He also is born out of the Adamic clay (which is an extract of the Fifth Essence—quintessence—of all creatures and of the whole world), ascending to Heaven and descending thence to Earth, and thus acquiring all power and might both in Heaven and Earth. Hence he is a Lord over all Animal, Vegetable, and Mineral Natures, and can act according to his pleasure, and the same with his influence—especially on man as the Microcosmus—if applied to man's Spirit of Life in an appropriate affinitative Vehicle.

But, as regards his other powers and influence over the metals, a means is necessary whereby to reduce, punish, and humble his rebellious people. Theophrastus here indicates gold as this means. Our Stone is first to conclude unity and friendship with the same, *i.e.*, they are both to be fused together.

Aurel. Augurell. says likewise, in his third book: "First mingle a little of the prepared medicament with the yellow metal, and thou wilt presently see the same take to itself the strength of the Blessed Powder.

"Or, when thou shalt have collected again, by great and difficult art, the teeming seed from the pure gold,

"Then quickly mix with it an equal portion of purple powder,

"And warm the same with gentle heat, simmering for two months;

"In which space of time thou mayst behold produced the whole series of colours,

"Which, otherwise, thou hadst marvelled to see in three years.

"As often as thou repeatest the operation again and again, so often shalt thou increase the virtue and quantity of thy powder."

But he conceals the important

point, for this fusion suffices not, if such molten matter be not heated during the proper time in a vessel with philosophical coction. For by this means the operator obtains full power over his Lord the King, thereupon reducing the subjects to obedience, as related by Dionysius Zacharius, a knack unknown to many operators, who have consequently not known how to set about the projection. For, although our Stone of itself colours, yet, according to Theophrastus, it does this less than when the Medium of Incorporation and Ingression of the Stone—*i.e.*, Fermentation—is added.

Different philosophers have used different Media, each according to his own opinion. Farrianus, Bernhardus, Roger Bacon, etc., etc., having some applied augmentation by means of repeated solution, others by fermentation. Use which you will; either will lead to the desired result. (*Vide Pandor.*, fol. 252.) But here I call a Ferment a Stone already complete in its elements in comparison with the metals: Even as the ferment of dough overcomes the dough, converting it into itself, so also this stone converts metals into itself, just as dough is changed and converted by its ferment, because it derives its origin from the same, and not from anything foreign. Thus, also, the Ferment of Metals is of their own substance, changing metals into itself. And since metals are generated from Mercury and Sulphur, therefore, also, this ferment is generated from them; and because this our Ferment is of the form, nature, and digestion of gold, therefore, it will reduce metals to the nature and digestion of gold. For the form of individuals of the same species is one alone.

As regards its third use, our Stone matures all immature precious stones, and brings them to their highest perfection. For this I refer you to others, being of opinion that such great gifts are given by God to man more to assist his neighbour by works of charity than to enrich himself. Would that man recognised the resources of Nature and God's wonderful wisdom in the implanting of such powers in His creation! Then, by means of this Igneous Sulphur or Lion's Blood, or Philosopher's Stone, he might attain the highest Rubinical Gradation of all Jewels, as well as the White Eagle, making large pearls of small ones; and, finally, might perform all philosophical works by the processes Theophrastus describes as digesting or putrefying, sublimating or distilling, calcining, extracting, fermenting, etc. These are the steps by which you may attain to wisdom and to Solomon's throne, on the right hand of which are found long life and the tree of life, and on the left, riches and honour. This is, says Theophrastus, the object of our art, viz., long life and the honourable maintenance of the same in this vale of tears.

Now will I briefly recapitulate to you the whole process: Take first thy golden Man, thy red Adamic earth. For this earth is the middle nature be-

The Natural Philosopher's Tincture. 257

tween Mercury and Metals, and the third thing composed of the same principles, Quicksilver and Sulphur. By noiseless metallic liquefaction of this earth the matter of its metallic ore acquires, by natural digestion, all the natures, virtues, and properties of the aforesaid principles, so that from it may be generated each and every metal, according to diversity of digestion; and to it is there nothing wanting but purification and complete digestion. This Red Adam lay in a warm bath that he may go to sleep. If he will not fall asleep, give him a good, strong, sleeping draught of his saturated liquor, which he loves to drink. Then, during his sleep, cut open his right side that the fair white woman, concealed within him, may come forth. When, now, this maiden has become marriageable, bring her to Adam—lying on his bed and sick with love—as his daughter, sister, and wife. Whereupon Adam will know the woman, and she will become pregnant. Take then this pregnant woman—letting the man go—and guard her well for ten months, until the day of her parturition. She will then bear her first-born son, whom she has conceived from her father's spirit, a young spiritual Adam, to whom no other man is equal in deeds and miracles, who—if daily fed with his young mother's milk—when he reaches man's estate, will subdue all his brethren, will deliver them from death, and bring them to eternal joy in the Kingdom of Honour, in which all creatures under heaven will rejoice with joy unspeakable. And, finally, the whole world will become full of gold, and pearls, and precious stones. For Solomon's vineyard bears him 1,000, and to those that keep the fruit thereof, 200.

Corollary concerning Hyle.

To say what Hyle is, is not puerile. Hyle is the primary matter and the Philosopher's Stone. Azoth is the seed of all metals, when it is extracted from Magnesia and Silver.

Hyle is the Beginning of all things, a confused mass and primary matter, which is neither moist nor dry, not earth nor water, not light nor darkness, not air nor fire.

Philosophers' Mercury is nothing else but a water or fire, both Elements having long been digested together with natural heat, resulting in a dry water. This Mercury is not common, but the Stars in the Firmament by their influence cause it to grow in the earth, the Quintessence of the Stars influencing the terrestrial Quintessence. You can drive them both into a water, and extract them therefrom, and they are to be observed in the Rainbow or Sun's reflection.

Another Corollary, by Conrad Poyselius,

An intimate friend of Theophrastus.

TAKE the strongest red subduer of men (cinnabar, red Mercurial earth) you can obtain, as it comes out of the earth. The Istrian, Candian, Hungarian, or Spanish kinds are the best. Distil the same three times, yet not too quickly, and put aside this thrice distilled spirit. Then of Red Royal Alum put several pounds into a vessel and calcine to blackness or greyness; pound also, and dissolve in warm water. Then extract the water *per Alembicum*, or evaporate in an open vessel till dry. Calcine again the residue, and again extract until it yields no more salt. Dissolve this salt, and coagulate for the third time until it ceases to yield a residue. Of this oil take one pound, place the same in a Waldburg or Hessian crucible, and set in a blast furnace until it fuses; add more oil if necessary. Allow it to fuse twenty-four hours in such furnace (if the crucible stand fire so long, even to three days); then take out and place in another crucible; fuse again, and repeat this operation a third time. The result will be a hard, green stone; pound the same, when warm, to pieces, place in a retort, and pour upon the stone of the above thrice distilled spirit three fingers' breadth. Set it, well closed up, upon hot ashes for three days and nights. Then the Vegetable Spirit, or White Eagle, will extract the Green Lion's rosy blood, and the superfluity and impurity will remain behind, partly as a scum and partly as a black, stinking oil or pitch. The scum swims upon the *Aqua* or *Spiritus Vitæ*, and the red blood upon that, like oil upon water. Pour the essentiated spirit into a glass, away from the scum and black residue (weigh the glass first).

The residual Stone can be farther desiccated until it have an oily or dry consistency. Use the same for Calculus,

Asthma, and other Tartaric diseases. The aforesaid Green Lion's Blood is the true Philosopher's Oil, above all aromas, always fixed and unalterable in fire. After remaining in the fire for a whole year it is still undiminished, looking like melted wax, as Geber testifies, saying he had seen nothing stable in fire except the viscous humidity, which is the root of all metals, and the true primary matter of Minerals, Animals, and Vegetables, as you, with God's help, will yourself experience.

Now, observe, when you have placed your Red Lion in the aforesaid weighed glass, distil the Eagle off in a bath, or over warm ashes. Collect the spirit by itself, putting away the phlegm, and you shall have the Lion's Blood in form of a fixed, stable, white salt. The Eagle goes off unwillingly, invisibly taking over the *Anima* or Soul in form of a sweet volatile salt, losing also its original scent. If you now will continue, and reach the desired goal, by God's help, take of the residual salt one part, and of the animated spirit three parts. Place in the aforesaid glass, in such a way that the third part of the same remain empty—as described by Poyselius in *Splendor Solis*. Seal hermetically, and, in God's Name, place in a vapour bath, giving it such warmth as an egg, or a child in the womb, requires. You will then behold within forty days how the soul, lying in this spirit, again assumes its body, and is the only medium for the re-uniting of body and spirit. When the matter begins to get black, then the conjunction goes on between the two, for this blackness is the body, or fixed salt, the passive thing, dominated by spirit and soul, and can be fused by no force of fire. As Bernhardus says: They wondrously love each other, and, although, in the beginning, the fixed body may be overcome by the spirit and soul, yet it is so strong, and of so incombustible a nature, that they cannot kill it, but when it finds the soul and spirit pressing it so hard, the Lion feels its old strength, and takes away from them the dominion. Before passive with respect to Soul and Spirit, it is now active as regards these, converting them into its own nature, and producing a true and clear substance, called the true, white Magnesia. But every intelligent artist may imagine for himself what various colours must be exhibited before this result is attained, how also it must be brought from one extreme to the other, viz., from white to black, and *vice versa*, which can only be done in several months. For Bernhardus says: "And I saw black clouds, but they lasted long; and, for the fire's sake, you must not alter the temperature until necessary, when it shall have coagulated into a greyish, white ash. Then you may increase the fire until the yellow appears, continuing to augment the temperature until you behold the desired perfect redness." But it is unnecessary here to state the whole procedure. Read with diligence the *Tinctura Physicorum* of Theophrastus Paracelsus, *Splendor Solis* of Ud. Poyselius, Raym.

Lullius, Bernhardus, Chrysippus, Farrianus, Chris. Parisiensis, Morienus, Rosarium Majus, The Epistle of Arnold de Villa Nova, Marlinum, the Book of Three Words, the First Part of the Breaking Day (not in print), and the second part thereof (in print). There you will find what is wanting here. Praise God, and succour the poor.

HERE FOLLOW
CERTAIN NOTABLE FACTS CONCERNING THE PHILOSOPHER'S STONE.

REBIS is making one thing of two. That is, philosophers' gold and silver—*i.e.*, the Philosopher's Stone—make a sulphur called philosophers' sulphur, and the secret of secrets. Gold generates gold, *i.e.*, when Medicine is to be prepared, then it is projected over gold or silver, and it is the required Medicine. Then the whole is projected over other, imperfect, bodies, and thus like generates like.

Philosophers' Mercury—*i.e.*, water out of the salt of metals—is none other than a body dissolved in water. *Aqua Vitæ* (Water of Life) is the same as Permanent Water, and is a spirit extracted from a body; it is called *Aqua Vitæ* and Quicksilver, and of it are all things made.

The spirit and soul are extracted from the body. The body was dead. Restore to it its soul! Then will it live and not die eternally, and then from these is made the stone which perfectly coagulates Mercury. The matter of the Stone is Philosophers' Salt, and Philosophers' Salt is Sulphur of imperfect metals.

The matter and form of the Stone: The form of the Stone is the same sulphur of gold or silver reduced to oil, with which the matter is incinerated, as aforesaid.

There are Four Degrees in the Regimen of Fire.

19. The first degree is that which permits of the hand being held to it, or is a temperature equal to that of a midsummer's day.

119. The second degree is that which permits the hand being held to the fire but a short time.

39. The third degree is that which produces no red glow, and causes not wood to carbonize in the heated sand.

40. The fourth degree is that which makes wood carbonize in the heated sand, yet produces not a red glow.

Concerning Salts.

TAKE of Lime of Metals 1 drachm, and of *Aqua Vitæ*, without phlegm, 4 drachms; cause them to boil gently forty-eight hours—or place in the Sun six days. After the sediment is deposited, pour off the clear liquid and distil. You will then have Salt of Metals, but not yet fermented; for it must be fermented with *Oleum Lunæ* to whiteness, and with *Oleum Solis* to redness. Likewise: of all things in the world—after first being reduced to ashes—there can be made a fixed Salt, fixing and really tinging every metallic body. All salts have the same efficacy as dissolved Mercury. Likewise, Incineration is effected thus: Take a white or red stone, at the same time somewhat congealed and powdered; place over a fire, and, when the said salt is a little heated, add a little of the powder, with sulphur or "Oleum Solis and Lunæ," continually, until the mixture be a sort of thick honey. Then take off the fire and colour; and thus do with all salts. Salts are softened by dissolution in fire, and then by alternate solution in and re-crystallization out of clear water.

Concerning Common Salt.
For the purification of Aqua Vitæ.

TAKE of Common Salt, prepared by solution and coagulation, and let it be many times dried; pour on it *Aqua Vitæ*, and distil with a strong fire, the more the better, and it will be rectified, dissolving gold. It ought to be distilled with salt at least three or four times.

Also: Pour out common salt, coagulate, and dissolve in common fresh water, repeating this until it be purified, and be obtained in crystalline form. Also: Let Antimony—and the other things not destroyed by combustion in the crucible—be dissolved in spirits of wine and distilled four days. Then extract therefrom the Salt and Oil.

NOTE: Philosophical Fire—which is called Nature and Soul—can be extracted from all natural things, and is of their nature and condition, because, in earth is earth, in water is water, in air is air, in fire is fire; neither has it causes of corruption nor contrary qualities.

Also: Of every Salt can a Tincture or Elixir be made, because an Elixir can be made of all things in the world, as has been said above, and hence also of Tartar, which Salt is a natural thing.

Also: The Philosopher says: The Spirit enters not except by water, *i.e.*, by Salt Water and the Regimen of fire, because whatever is dissolved out of Salts is done over a gentle fire, and whatever is dissolved by means of Salt Water remains, and is not altered. Hence, if you would be enriched, prepare Common Salt and Alkali, and reduce them into pure, sweet water, which is preparative and incerative water, in which—if thou shalt have decocted the whitened spirits—it will rectify and whiten the same, extinguishing therein all blackness.

To be noted: Prepare Salts; make them liquid and commiscible with bodies, and—if thou wouldst be enriched—prepare especially *Sal Alpoli*. For its property is to retain volatile things, and hence they are more quickly liquefied and collected. For, whatever has been dissolved out of Salts over a slow fire, should afterwards be distilled over three times with a very slow fire. The residue in the still should be removed and preserved, and the said water be again re-distilled until perfectly pure water passes over. In the fifth distillation the water will be pure, and then it is finished, as the Philosopher says. When you obtain water from air, and air from fire, and fire from earth, then you have the whole Art.

From the above it is patent that salt enters not a body, neither are bodies mixed with it, unless the salt be made liquable, nor are those complexionable unless the saltness be purged away. Then will it be an Elixir, a most limpid Condiment, like the Coagulum of Milk. For the dryness of salt is the calcinative and parcher of all bodies and spirits. But the property of water is mild, purifying and rectifying bodies and spirits. Take care, for it is a light sort, that thou mayst collect gold and silver perfectly pure, for it rectifies and perfects whitened spirits.

By boiling thou mayst obtain many things wherewith to coagulate Mercury and change it into perfect silver. Hence the Philosopher: If Quicksilver be joined to its own kind, it will doubtless flee away, but if *quick* when fleeing, suffering another union with water, it bears fire and the hammer.

Praise God in thy soul for what I have said, and praised be God who hath placed His Wisdom in Salt! Work with the same and thou shalt prosper.

Here follow some Philosophical Rules or Canons concerning the Philosopher's Stone.

WHAT we seek is here or nowhere.

1. Canon: The nearly perfect is easily brought to perfection.

2. Imperfect things by no art can put on perfection, unless first purged from impure Sulphur and earthly grossness, which are mixed with Mercury and Sulphur; then are they accounted a perfect Medicine.

3. It is wholly impossible to render imperfect bodies fixed without the Sulphur and Spirit of the perfect ones.

4. The Philosophers' *Cælum* (Heaven) reduces all metals to their primary matter, *i.e.*, to Mercury.

5. Those attempting to reduce metals into Mercury without *Cælum*

Philosophicum, or metallic *Aqua Vitæ*, or Tartar of the same, are greatly deceived, since the impurity out of other solutions swimming in Mercury is perceived by their own eyes.

6. Nothing is perfectly fixed, except it be indissolubly joined to a fixed substance.

7. Fusible gold may be mutated, and changed into blood.

8. To render silver stable it must be reduced neither to a powder nor to water—for this would destroy it utterly—but it must of necessity be reduced to Quicksilver.

9. Silver cannot be transmuted into gold (except *Physica Tinctura*), unless it be reduced to liquid Mercury. The same is to be said of the other metals.

10. Imperfect bodies, as well as silver, are endowed with perfection, and converted into pure gold; and this is done with white or red sulphur by the virtue of a suitable fire.

11. Every imperfect body is brought to perfection by reduction into Mercury,

after decoction with sulphurs in an appropriate fire. For out of the same are generated gold and silver; and they are deceived and labour in vain, who try to make gold and silver in any other way.

12. Sulphur of Iron is the best, for this, joined to Sulphur of Gold, brings forth a certain Medicine.

13. No gold is generated, except it have first been silver.

14. Nature compounds and prepares its minerals by a gradual process: and thus at length from one root it procreates all metals to the last limit of metals, which is gold.

15. Mercury corrupts gold, changing it into Mercury, and rendering it volatile.

16. The Stone is composed of Sulphur and Mercury.

17. If the preparation of Mercuries be not taught by an experienced artificer, it cannot be learnt from books.

18. The preparation of Mercury for the philosophical menstruum is called Mortification.

19. The practice of this great work remains our Grand Secret or Arcanum, and unless it be revealed Divinely, or by artificers, or in experiments, it also can never be learnt from books.

20. Sulphur and Mercury are the ingredients of the stone. Hence a knowledge of Mercury is necessary, to select the best Mercury for the speedy perfecting of the Stone.

21. A certain Mercury is latent in every body, but the art of extraction is most difficult.

22. Mercury can only be changed into gold or silver by an abbreviation of the long process.

23. Congealing and fixing necessitate but one and the same operation, in the same vessel, and with the same substance.

24. What congeals and fixes Mercury also colours the same, in one and the same process.

25. There are four degrees of fire to be observed in the process. In the first Mercury dissolves; in the second

Sulphur dries up Mercury; in the third and fourth Mercury is fixed.

26. Things radically mingled in their minutest parts afterwards become inseparable, like snow mixed with water.

27. Different Simple Substances exposed to putrefaction give different products.

28. It necessarily behoves form and matter to be of the same species.

29. Homogeneous Sulphur is of that Mercurial Nature which produces gold and silver, not in the form in which they are perceived by the eyes, but in which Mercury is dissolved.

30. Without Philosophical Solution of Gold in Mercury, there cannot be extracted from gold the certain fixed unctuosity which acts the part of a ferment generating gold and silver. The same is effected by a short method described by Geber.

31. Metals resolved into Mercury are again reduced to their original form by admixture of a small portion of this

ferment; otherwise they permanently retain Mercurial form.

32. *Cœlum*, or Tartar of Philosophers, which reduces all metals into Mercury, is metallic philosophers' *Aqua Vitæ*.

33. Sulphur and Mercury consist of the same homogeneous nature.

34. The Philosophers' Stone is none other than gold and silver endued with a more than perfect tincture and excellence.

35. Gold and silver contain in themselves a superabundance of riches, which—by preparation and digestion—should be changed into a ferment, whereby the mass may be multiplied.

36. The greatest extremities in Mercury are two, viz., exceeding crudeness, and exceedingly exquisite decoction.

37. Philosophers hold it as an axiom that every dry thing quickly drinks up the humidity of its own species.

38. Lime of Silver alterated quickly drinks up its Mercury, the fundament of the minerals of Philosophers.

39. Sulphur is the Soul, Mercury the Matter.

40. Mercury, placed with the sulphur of imperfect bodies, is coagulated into an imperfect body, being transmuted into that imperfect metallic species, the sulphur of which is coagulated and concreted.

41. It is wholly impossible to make gold and silver with the sulphur of imperfect bodies. For nothing can excel that which it contains within itself.

42. Mercury is the feminine seed and menstruum of all metals, suitably prepared by the good operator's Art. For, by the projection of the great work, it receives and transmits the qualities of all metals, even to gold.

43. As Red Tincture is elicited by the ferment of gold alone, Mercury can be animated only by the white ferment of silver.

44. The Philosophers' work can be carried on without much labour or expense at all times, in every place, and by all, if only the true and sufficient matter be forthcoming.

45. The sulphurs of gold and silver stand the spirits of their species.

46. The sulphurs of gold and silver are the true seeds, feminine or masculine, of the Stone.

47. Everything conferring the virtue of stability and permanence necessarily possesses this virtue itself.

48. The tincture imparting perfection to the imperfect derives this perfection from the fount of gold and silver.

49. Those are deceived who accept Venus as sulphur.

50. Nothing has been granted by Nature to Venus which answers for the great Spagyric work, or which will serve in the making of gold and silver.

51. NOTE. Gold converted into Mercury before conjunction with the menstruum, can be neither spirit, nor ferment, nor sulphur, and is good for nothing.

52. The work brought to an end by reiteration cannot again be made hot.

53. In abbreviating the work perfect bodies should be reduced to liquid

Mercury and dry water, when they will easily assimilate the ferment.

54. The preparation of Mercury effected by sublimation is the more excellent, and by it (after revivification) is amalgamation more easily and better carried out.

55. The Soul cannot impress the Form, except by intervention of the Spirit, which is gold transmuted into Mercury.

56. Mercury receives the form of gold through the medium of the Spirit.

57. Gold resolved into Mercury is Spirit and Soul.

58. Philosophers' Sulphur, Tincture, Ferment, designate one and the same thing.

59. Common Mercury is the equal of and nearly approaches the Nature and Similitude of all other Mercuries.

60. Ferment renders Mercury heavier.

61. If Common Mercury be **not** animated, it is unsuitable for philosophical purposes.

62. The Soul is already impressed on Mercury properly mortified.

63. Gold may be prepared in a ferment, so that one part shall animate ten parts of Common Mercury, but this work has no end.

64. Mercury of imperfect bodies holds a middle place between common Mercury and that of perfect bodies; but the art of extraction is most difficult.

65. Since Common Mercury, by projection of the Stone, can be changed into gold or silver, it can be made equal to all Mercuries of the Bodies.

66. Animated Common Mercury is the greatest secret.

67. The Mercuries of all metals, by abbreviation of the work, are changed into gold or silver.

68. A humid and gentle heat is called by the name of Egyptian fire.

69. It is worthy to be noted that Luna is not the mother of common silver, but a certain Mercury endued with the quality of the celestial moon.

Philosophical Rules or Canons. 285

70. The Metallic Luna (silver) is of masculine nature.

71. Common Mercury, from cold, assumes the nature of a sterile woman.

72. The Mercuries of semi-minerals bear in their nature a similitude to Luna.

73. All things are produced from Sol and Luna, viz., from two substances.

74. Male and female—*i.e.*, Sol and Mercury—coalesce into one.

75. Common Mercury, without preparation, is unsuitable for the work.

76. Four parts of Mercury and one of Sol—*i.e.*, of the ferment—constitute the true marriage of male and female.

77. The solution is complete when Sol is resolved into Mercury.

78. Without putrefaction is no solution perfected.

79. Putrefaction extends and continues even unto whiteness.

80. The great arcanum is the maturing of the spirit, by which is prepared the menstruum, for in the same is Sol dissolved.

81. Mercury dissolves gold into water of its own form, *i.e.*, into liquid Mercury.

82. Dissolution is the principle of congelation.

83. Gold transmuted into liquid Mercury, remains but a short time in that form.

84. Ferment desiccates Mercury, rendering it heavier and stable.

85. Sol (gold) is called the Philosopher's Fount.

86. Matter, by force of putrefaction, is converted into pulp or mud, which is the principle of coagulation.

87. The long method is the open secret of Philosophy, but it is a veil and an evasion.

88. There is a certain short method by which the Sulphur is removed from gold and silver, whereby every Mercury is permanently changed into gold and silver.

89. When matter attains blackness of colour, the second degree of heat must be applied.

90. Philosophers' Laton is the similitude of fire, for that alone perfects and excels all things.

91. Poison and stench are removed by fire, without other addition, and it alone cleanses all things.

92. Fire, by its penetrative and acute virtue, purifies and matures a hundred times more than any water.

93. When heat is extinguished in the vegetation and generation of any thing, death suddenly invades the growing substance.

94. The Spirit is Heat.

95. Matter, when brought to whiteness, refuses to be corrupted and destroyed.

96. All corruption of matter is marked by deadly poison.

97. The glass, or vessel, is called the "Mother."

98. The virtue of Sulphur is not extensive, except to a certain limit of proportion, neither can it exceed an unlimited weight.

99. The question is to be observed,

wherefore Philosophers call the matter of the Stone a Menstruum.

100. Sulphur merits the name of form, but menstruum that of matter.

101. Menstruum represents the small and inferior elements, viz., Earth and Water—Sulphur, the two superior ones, viz., Fire and Air, as the Masculine Agent.

102. Thou canst not hatch the chicken by breaking the egg-shell; similarly, thou canst have no result by opening the vessel and exposing the matter to the air.

103. The Calcination, by means of Mercury in a blast furnace, excels others.

104. The Philosophers' mode of speaking must be diligently noted. By sublimation they mean the dissolution of bodies into Mercury. By the first degree of fire they mean that which the second operation follows, viz., the inspissation (thickening) of Mercury with Sulphur. The third is the fixation of Mercury into a perfect and dissolved body.

105. Infinite is the number of the erring who admit not that Mercury, as regards its form, when mixed with amalgamated chalk of perfect bodies, is the subject and matter of the Stone.

106. White Medicine is brought to perfection in the third degree of fire, which must not be exceeded lest the work—for whiteness—be destroyed.

107. The fourth degree of fire produces a red matter, when appear divers colours.

108. It is necessary that whiteness, not yet brought to highest redness, should remain imperfect, both as regards the white and the red tincture. Therefore it is left dead until it ends in perfect redness.

109. After the fifth degree of perfecting fire, the matter acquires new virtues.

110. The work attains not perfection, unless the medicine have been incerated and rendered fusible like wax.

111. The process of ceration is repeated three times on a quantity of

the Binary Mercury, which produces the Stone.

112. The inceration of white Medicine is effected with white water or Mercury animated by Luna; but the inceration of Red Tincture with Mercury animated by Sol.

113. After inceration it suffices for the matter to remain in the form of pulp or paste.

114. Repeat the inceration until it stands the perfect test.

115. If the Mercury, by which the Medicine is incerated, escapes as a vapour, the work has failed.

116. Medicine, rightly incerated, explains to thee the enigma of the king returning from the fountain.

117. Sol—when converted into its primary water, or Mercury, by means of Mercury—if it become cold, causes the work to perish.

118. Philosophers, taking matter prepared and concocted by Nature, reduce it to its primary matter, since everything returns to that whence it

derives its origin, even as snow is inseparably resolved into water.

119. The Wise reduce years to months, months to weeks, weeks to days.

120. The first decoction of Mercury—which Nature effects—is the sole cause of its simple perfection, beyond which of itself it can rise very little; and it is meet to assist its simplicity by sowing our gold in its proper earth; this is none other than pure Mercury, which Nature has digested a little, and not perfectly.

121. But by this second decoction Mercury becomes multiplied in virtue tenfold beyond its primary nature.

122. But the Stone Mercury is produced by repeated decoctions and mixing with Sol. Therefore, for this cause, man and woman follow twice.

123. By addition of Sol to Mercury it is converted into sulphur, and then by decoction into the Philosopher's Stone.

124. He who contemplates Philoso-

phers' Mercury but for a few moments, the same neither knows nor understands it.

125. Every Mercury, of whatever origin, exhibits the matter of the Stone, when treated in the right manner.

126. Everything from which Mercury may be elicited is a subject of Philosophical Medicine.

127. Those who understand the Philosophers' Writings literally greatly err when they assert their Mercury to be One.

128. One Mercury exceeds the other in greater heat, dryness, decoction, purity, perfection; it ought to be prepared without corruption or loss of form, and to be purged from superfluities. In this consist the treasure and mystery of the Stone.

129. If the preparation of Common Mercury were known to students of Philosophy, no other Philosophers' Mercury, nor Metallic *Aqua Vitæ*, nor other Mercurial Water of the Stone, need be sought, since the preparation of

Common Mercury includes all these things.

130. Every Mercury of Metals and Minerals may, by successive stages, be raised, through the qualities of all other Mercuries, to the excellence of the Solar Body, and thence also be reduced to the degree and virtue of any metallic body one may please.

131. Common Mercury, before legitimate preparation, is not Philosophers' Mercury, but after preparation it is called Mer. Phil., containing within itself the true method and way of extracting Mercury from other metals—it is, as it were, the beginning of the great work.

132. Prepared Common Mercury is held to be Metallic *Aqua Vitæ*.

133. Passive Mercury and Menstruum should on no account lose the external form of Mercury.

134. Those who (for the philosophical work), in place of liquid Mercury, use sublimate, or calcined powder, or precipitate, are deceived, and err greatly.

135. Those who—for the perfecting

of the philosophical work—resolve Mercury into clear water, err greatly.

136. To compound and make Mercury of limpid water is in the power of Nature alone.

137. In the Great Physical Work it is necessary that crude Mercury resolve Sol into Mercury.

138. If Mercury be reduced into water, it dissolves Sol into water, and, in the work of the Stone, it is highly necessary that it be dissolved into Mercury.

139. It behoves the Sperma and Menstruum to have servile external forms.

140. According to Philosophers, we should imitate Nature. Were, therefore, Menstruum dry, solution would be hoped for in vain.

141. The seed of the Stone should be in form similar to metals.

142. It is highly necessary to choose that seed of Philosophical Medicine which bears Common Mercury.

143. It is the mystery of all mys-

teries of the Stone to know Mercury to be the matter, menstruum, and form of perfect bodies.

144. Mercury, of itself, brings nothing of moment to gradation.

145. Mercury is the Element of Earth, in which a seed of Sol must be implanted.

146. The seed of gold effects, not only the multiplying of quantity, but also of virtue.

147. Perfected Mercury, for the generation of the work, has need of a female.

148. Each Mercury is derived from, and participates in, two Elements—Crude, from water and earth; Decocted, from fire and air.

149. If any one wish to prepare and exalt Mercury into a Metal, let him add a little ferment, whereby it may be raised to the required metallic degree.

150. The highest mystery of the whole Work is the Physical Dissolution into Mercury, and the reduction into primary matter.

151. The dissolution of Sol should be effected by Nature, not by handiwork.

152. Sol, when joined or married to its Mercury, will be in the form of Sol, but the major preparation will be in chalk.

153. It is an open question among Sages whether *Mercurius Lunæ* conjoined with *Mercurius Solis* can be obtained in place of philosophical menstruum.

154. *Mercurius Lunæ* has a masculine nature. But two males can generate as little as two females.

155. When eliciting the Elixir, the purest substance of Mercury must be chosen.

156. He who wishes to be employed, let him be employed in the solution and sublimation of the two Luminaries.

157. Gold imparts a golden, silver a silvery colour. But he who knows how to colour Mercury with Sol or Luna, the same attains to the Arcanum.

HERE FOLLOWS
AN ANONYMOUS TREATISE
CONCERNING THE
PHILOSOPHER'S STONE.

MY noble and dear Son, in order that I may communicate to you, in the briefest manner, my knowledge of the right, true, philosophical Stone, now know and understand that this Stone is composed of two things, Body and Spirit, to wit, male and female Seed, that is, Mercurial Water and *Corpus Solis*, as may be read in all philosophical works.

And it is the general opinion that Mercury—free from foreign admixture—should first be dissolved in a spiritual water, called by philosophers primary matter of metals, *Liquor Lunæ*, *Aqua Vitæ*, Quintessence, and a fiery burning water or spirit, with which water, or primary matter, the metals are delivered and freed from their rigid, frozen bonds, and are dissolved into their primary nature, like mercurial water itself. Hence philosophers, in their books, have illustrated their meaning by saying that ice dissolves into water by means of heat, because it was water before its coagulation. For everything is reducible to its primary condition. Therefore, also, philosophers have written that the species or forms of metals cannot be changed into gold and silver before being first reduced to their primary matter.

With respect to this regeneration of metals, observe well, my son, that the same can take place by means of the primary matter of metals—*i.e.*, mercurial water alone, and through nothing else in the world. For this water has the greatest affinity to metallic nature, so that—after equal mixture—it can never be separated from the same.

Therefore have philosophers, in the *Turba* and other books, indicated this water, saying: Nature rejoices in Nature, Nature preserves, improves, unites with, reduces, and exalts Nature. Hence it is necessary to know how to prepare the Blessed Water, which water is a fiery penetrating spirit, a philosophical water, and the hidden key of this Art. For, verily, without this water all Alchemy is vain. Therefore, my son, remember that the whole Fundament of the Philosopher's Stone consists in bringing to a new birth the primary matter of metals —*i.e.*, Mercurial Water, the perfect *Corpus Solis*—that it be born again by water and of the spirit, just as Christ says: "Except a man be born again by water and the Spirit, he cannot see the Kingdom of God." So also here in this art, I tell thee, my son: Except *Corpus Solis* be sowed, all else is vain, and there will be no fruit. Even as Christ says: "Except the Seed fall into the earth and die, it shall bear no fruit." When, now, *Corpus Solis* has been born again through water and the Spirit, it grows up a purified, astral, everlasting, immortal body, bringing much fruit and multiplying after the manner of vegetables.

Concerning this Roger Bacon says: I declare unto you that if the *Astrum* (Star) turn its inclination to, and impress it on, this clarified gold body, it can nevermore lose its virtue and power. For the body is perfect, composed of, and agreeable to, all the elements. Therefore, my son, let him not attempt this Art who knows not of this new birth in Nature, and this bringing forth of metals through the water and spirit of primary matter. For, believe me, all else is useless, vain, and deceiving. Hence philosophers have written that: "Everything brings forth its like; and what a man sows that shall he reap."

Therefore says the Philosopher Richard, the Englishman: Sow gold and silver, that they, by means of Nature, may bring forth fruit.

Hence, my son, for thy work seek no other body but gold, as others are all imperfect. For gold is the most perfect of bodies, enlightening and vivifying all others, stable in fire, possessing a fixed, incombustible root; and, as Bacon testifies, one can alter nothing in the nobility and perfection of gold, it being free from all natural ferment, and no substance in the world is more perfect. Therefore, says Isaac the Philosopher: "The Stone can only be extracted from a perfect body, the most perfect in the world. For, were this body not perfect, how should we extract therefrom a Stone having power to give life to all mortal, to purify all corrupt, to soften all hard, and harden all soft bodies? Verily, it were impossible to extract so excellent a Stone from an imperfect body! Although many attempt it, yet are they fools." Therefore, my son, understand that the red, philosophical, Sulphur is a gold, as Richard testifies, and King Calid also states: "Our Sulphur is no common Sulphur, but is of Mercurial Nature, stable, fleeing not water." Other Philosophers also bear witness that their Red Sulphur is gold.

Now, my son, the Sages say in their books that common gold and silver are not their gold or silver, since theirs are living, while the common are dead, and therefore incapable of imparting to others the perfection they themselves are wanting in. Now, my son, those words of the Philosophers are true; it is impossible for common gold or silver to perfect other imperfect bodies, except—as I have said before—the *Corpus Solis* and *Lunæ* be born again through the Water and Spirit of Primary Matter, and arise as a transfigured, spiritual, clarified, eternally fixed, subtle, penetrating body, which afterwards shall have power to perfect and multiply imperfect bodies. Therefore have our Philosophers said: For this reason are such labours undertaken on our Stone, that its tincture may be improved, for our Stone must be much more subtle and decocted than common gold and silver. Bernhardus says: "We therefore take this body as created by Nature. But it is necessary to more than perfect the masculine body by natural art, in order that in its more-than-perfection it may render the imperfect perfect, by its superabundant fertility in weight, colour, and substance. And, if its perfection were not greater in degree than that imparted by Nature, what use would our time of nine-and-a-half months be?" Hence Arnoldus de Villa Nova, in his Epistle concerning our Stone, says: "The power and virtue and nature of gold and silver are in the Stone, else no gold or silver could be made. But the gold and silver in our Stone are better than the common, since the former are living. Hence Philosophers call the Stone their gold and silver, because the same are in it potentially and essentially, but not visibly." Euclides says: "A perfect thing is unchangeable. For example, bread. Bread, baked and kneaded, is perfect in degree and nature, has attained its final form, and of it can be made nothing but bread. Thus also with philosophical gold. Hence it is impossible to perfect other bodies with common gold, except the perfect *Corpus Solis* be again dissolved into its primary matter, whereupon it is converted by our Art into a veritable Ferment or Tincture, philosophers saying the process is not finished until Sol and Luna are joined into one body. My son, understand here the *Luna Metaphorica*, not the literal, since philosophers explain Luna to be of a cold, moist nature, giving the same definition also to Mercury. Hence by Luna is understood Mercury, or Mercurial Water, or primary matter, which is the Philosophers' Luna, or *Liquor Lunæ* of the *Clangor Buccinæ*.

Now, my son, you have a short explanation why it is impossible to do anything in this Art, except we reduce perfect bodies, by philosophical fire or mercurial water, to their primary nature, which primary nature is a Sulphureous Water, and not Quicksilver as Sophists assert. For the primary matter of metals is not Quicksilver, but a sticky, sulphureous steam, and a viscous water, in which water are united the three principles, Salt, Sulphur, and Mercury. Therefore it is necessary to know the Blessed Water of Mercury, or celestial, supernatural fire, by which bodies are dissolved and fused. This knowledge is the greatest secret and is revealed by God alone. For the Philosopher Bacon says: God Almighty has created man above Nature and all creatures—although man is of Nature, excepting the Breath of God breathed into him at the creation—and he shall be the lord of Nature's works. This Divine Spirit fashions the mind and thoughts of man, teaching him to perceive the first principles of Nature. The inspired Apostle, St. Peter, tells us that the Elements will melt with fervent heat, that the Earth and its works shall consume therein, and a new world shall be born, beautiful and good, as is described in the Apocalypse. Thence the Philosopher concludes—like St. Peter—that the elemental world can only be destroyed by fire. Therefore, remember in this Art that fire is the instrument, according to Nature's example, and, next, understand further that this water, whereby *Corpus Solis* (gold)—which, as Roger Bacon testifies, is a world perfectly created—is burnt, destroyed, and melted, is not a common fire—since common fire can neither burn nor destroy gold—but a supernatural, inconsumable fire, which alone has power to burn gold and release it from its hard, rigid bonds. Also, my son, understand that this supernatural fire, possessing such power over gold and other metallic bodies, is alone the spiritual, sulphureous, fiery water of Mercury, in which *Corpus Solis* is fused and burnt; and, out of this melting and destruction, is again born and created a new world, and the Heavenly Jerusalem, *i.e.*, an eternal, clarified subtle, penetrating, stable body, which can penetrate and perfect all other bodies. Hence Bacon says: "Just as a supernatural or elemental fire is that which disintegrates and fuses the elements of the whole world, and as the new Creation will be born from the mortal, molten elements, and will be an eternal Creation; even so has the Holy Trinity in the Celestial Stone also revealed to us a supernatural fire. My son, philosophers in their books have concealed this Fire, describing it in parables and by countless names; in particular, they call it Mary's Bath, and a horse-dung, Menstruum, Urine, Milk, Blood, *Aqua Vitæ, &c.*" Concerning this Fire, Bernhardus says: "Make a vaporous fire, steady, digesting, not strong, subtle, airy, clear, condensed, inconsumable, penetrating, and equable." And he continues: "Verily, I tell thee, all wisdom is in this fire, for the said vaporous fire performs all things." Hence he directs us to copy his words concerning this fire, word for word. Therefore, a wise man will easily understand that such words refer not to a common, but to a supernatural fire. Hence Maria says: "The Element Water makes white and melts bodies." Concerning the preparation of this fire—which he calls menstruum—Raymundus Lullius says in his books (which are *Testam Test. Noviss., Codicil., Anima Metallorum, Lux Mercuriorum, Liber Mercurius, Liber de Secretis Naturæ, de Quintessentia*, and especially in *Elucidarium Testamenti*, chap. iv.: That it is not of men but of Angels to reveal this Celestial Fire, for therein is the greatest secret; and he indicates in figurative words that such Fire of the Sages is composed of horsedung and living chalk. What living chalk represents I will explain elsewhere. As to "horsedung," I have already indicated that it is the water of primary matter, for the same is warm and moist. But it is not common horsedung, as many ignorantly imagine. Therefore the Philosopher Alanus says: "Philosophers have named the moist fire horsedung, in which moisture is retained the latent heat; and it is the property of the fire in the horse's belly not to destroy gold, but to multiply it by reason of its moisture." Alchidonius says: "Verily our medicine is to be hidden in horsedung, which is the Sages' Fire." And Alanus: "Dear son, be diligent in disintegrating, and the same must take place in gentle heat, that is, in tepid horsedung." So also Arnold de Villa Nova, chap. 9 (Concerning Heat), says that "the heat of horsedung is its fire." And Alphidius: "Let it be boiled and buried in the warmth of horsedung." Also Aristoteles: "The Earth, or body, will rejoice in no strength unless sublimated by horsedung." Hermes: "Roast and boil it in the warmth of the horse's belly." And Morienus: "If thou find not what thou seekest in horsedung, spare thyself further expense." Arnoldus: "And seek no other fire but this, for this is the Sages' Fire and Furnace. This water dissolves and calcines all metals, and fuses them white and red." Therefore say the *Turba* and Senior: Our water is the fire, and our water is stronger than all fire, making out of gold a pure spirit, which natural fire cannot do, although natural fire also belongs to it. For our water, penetrating the natural metal, converts it into primary water, and afterwards into an earth or powder, which burns gold more than natural fire. Hence Calid says: "It is verily a fire burning and destroying all things." But philosophers have concealed the preparation of this philosophical water or fire, *i.e.*, Mercurial Water. Raymundus Lullius has written most plainly concerning the same: "And it will first be necessary to purify Mercury from its external moisture and earthy earthiness, but not with pernicious, destructive things, whereby its noble, fruitful, teeming nature would be destroyed." Avicenna, Arnold Geber, Raym., in the Codicill., and others, assert that Mercury is best purified by the sublimation of common, prepared salt. By treating the sublimate with hot water, the spirit of salt is dissolved out. Dry the sublimate, and mix with Tartaric Salt. Heat several times in a retort, when the Mercury will distil over vivified, and in this way will be somewhat freed from external moisture and impurities. This purgation, says Bernhardus, is not injurious, since the hot water and salt penetrate it not. But, my son, understand that Mercury cannot be thoroughly purified by external treatment, since it is a homogeneous, indivisible substance, "whose impurities penetrate its inmost being, and can therefore be removed by no sublimation." Hence another means must here be sought, viz., that of dissolving purified Quicksilver and loosing its natural bonds, and changing it into its primary form, which is a sulphureous, spiritual water. Bacon and Raymundus Lullius both testify that unless purification and solution be effected, the menstruum will not be worth a fig.

When now Mercury is freed from its bonds and resolved into its primary water, we can inwardly purify it, and, by distillation, separate the spirit from the water and earthy earthiness. Concerning which separation the philosophers have written mysteriously, and in particular have discovered the same figuratively in the distillation of wine. For in vinous distillation we see that the spirit of wine is mixed with much water and earthy impurity. But, by artificial distillation, the spirit can be separated from phlegmatic wateriness and earthy impurity, a residue remaining. From which residue, after calcination, is extracted a white salt which—added to the spirit, and repeatedly distilled—produces a spirit mightily strengthened and sharpened by this salt of nitre. Verily the above is a figurative description given us by philosophers, which we should follow in the preparation of Mercurial Water. Since the same—after disintegration and solution, *i.e.*, similarly to wine—can, by sublimation, be separated from the water or phelgm, rectified, etc. And, verily, no one has written more clearly concerning the preparation of this Mercurial Water than Raymund. Lullius, viz., in "Test. Noviss.," also in the "Liber Mercuriorum (Test. I.)," etc., etc., in which he plainly enough declares that, after putrefaction, distillation, and separation of philosophical spirits of wine, the spiritual water is again mingled with its earth, and distilled over the alembic, further explaining how the said philosophical wine, or menstruum, is sharpened and strengthened with a salt.

This Water Menstruum, or philosophical spirits of wine, therefore, dissolves its own body, or animated Mercury, into the primary matter, or water, by which it can then be indefinitely multiplied with the help of putrefaction and distillation. A. de Villa Nova writes concerning this water thus: "There is a crumbling substance containing a fatty mixture, from which substance the master separates Philosophers' Liquid, which is suitable for the work and exceedingly clear. Therein dwells the Fifth Essence (Quintessence) Metallically, and the same has affinity to metals, and in it is the Tincture to be brought together, as being a perfect metal, for it has within itself the nature of Quicksilver and of Sulphur."

I will here (although forbidden) quote "Rosarius Philosophorum" concerning the distillation of this menstruum, or water: "In the distillation of the spirit care must be taken, and the vessels in which thou purifiest thy spirit must be of glass, that the spirit find not a place to flow out, by reason of its quickness. For if the Red Spirit escape, the Artist labours in vain. Artists call the Red Spirit a blood, and menstruum; therefore take heed with thy vessels that thou collect the dry spirit with its blood by itself in a receptacle, without diminution of its strength, so that thou mayst store up the same for future use." But, in distillation, seeing is more than writing. Hence nobody should be a master before having been a disciple. Therefore be careful in the work. Place a receptacle beneath, and distil first—with gentle heat—the element of water. Set the same aside, substituting another receptacle; close well the joints, that the spirit escape not, and increase the fire a little. Then will rise in the helmet, and distil over, a dry, yellow spirit; keep the fire steady while the helmet is yellow. Afterwards, when the helmet begins to get red, increase the fire slowly, and keep it so until the Red Spirit and the Blood have quite distilled out, passing through the helmet like clouds in the air. When the Red Spirit has distilled over, the helmet will become white. Then cease quickly, and thou hast in the receptacle the two elements, Air and Fire, and thus hast extracted the right dry spirit, and hast separated the pure from the impure. Behold, thou hast now the primary matter of metals, having thus separated the pure from the impure! Behold, thou hast now the water in which all metals have their origin, which is of all metals the root! Hence are they dissolved into water, even as frozen ice is resolved into water, since the same clearly was water in the first place. Therefore marvel not at this, for all things upon earth have their root in water. Oh, how many are there that, working, never think of this root, which is the key of the whole work? The same immediately dissolves bodies, is father and mother, opens out and locks up, and reduces bodies to their primary matter. It dissolves bodies, coagulating itself with them, and the Spirit of the Lord is led forth upon the Water, *i.e.*, the strength of the spirit is seen to be active therein, and this takes place when the body is placed in this water. And the philosopher adds: " Behold the base thing with which our Sanctuary has been opened! For it is a thing well known by everyone; yet, he who understands it not finds it seldom or never. The wise man keeps it, the fool throws it away, and its reduction is easy to the initiated." But, my son, the freeing of this Stone, or Mercury, from its natural bonds, and its resolution into primary water, is the greatest and most secret of mysteries. And, without it, all else were vain, for we could not separate or extract the right spirit or Watery Essence that dissolves bodies. And this dissolving has been kept secret by all philosophers, and they have placed the revealing of the same in God's hand, and have cursed the man who should publish it. Hence they have spoken briefly and with subtlety of this resolution, that the same might remain hidden from the ignorant. But, thou, my son, observe that such resolution of Animated Mercury can hardly be effected without the proper means (coagulation). But, observe further, that here are not to be used sophistical means, like those used by ignorant fools who, reducing common Mercury to water by sophistical contrivances, vainly imagine they possess the true water. They sublime Mercury with all manner of corrosive salts and vitriols (whereby the sublimate generates Spirits of Salt), and, afterwards, dissolve the sublimate into water in a bath, cellar, and otherwise. They also make it into water by means of Salmiac, herbs, soaps, aquafortis, with strange vessels, and such like sophistical methods, which are, altogether, great phantasy, foolishness, and vanity; and then they imagine they can again separate such things from Mercurial Water, and thus obtain the true water desired of philosophers. But all is false, and they find not what they seek. And the cause of their failure is their neglect of the teaching of philosophers, who plainly declare that it should be mixed with no foreign matter. Bernhardus says in his Epistle: When Mercury is dried by Salt, Aquafortis, or other thing, it is no more suitable for philosophical work; for, dried by Salts, Alums, and Aquafortis, it dissolves not any more. But, thou, my son, remember what I now tell thee, and what philosophers have, in their books, revealed to the understanding, that this water is to be prepared with no foreign matter in the world, but alone by Nature, with Nature, and out of Nature. These are to the understanding plain, clear words, which I will not in this place explain more at length, but will embody them in a Treatise. Yet as an aid to memory I give you the following verses:

Take it fresh, pure, living white and clear,
Then bind firmly both hands and feet
With the very strongest cords,
That it suffocate and die.
In the closed House of Putrefaction,
According to Nature's example,
Let the same Nature dissolve it
Into pure and beautiful primary matter.
Then shall it be a living, spiritual Fount,
Flowing from Heaven pure and clear;
Eating its own flesh and blood,
Whereby it is multiplied.

He who, by Divine Aid, has attained this Blessed Water, let him praise God; for he holds in his hands the key with which he can unlock the treasure houses containing gold, silver, precious stones, honour, power, and health. This Blessed Water is by philosophers called Pluto's Daughter, having power over all treasures. She is also called the white, pure, tender, undefiled Virgin Bega, without whom no bringing forth nor mingling can take place. Therefore have philosophers married this pure, tender Virgin to Gabricus, that she might bear fruit; and Gabricus, having known her, died. Bega, by reason of her great love, swallowed and devoured him, as Aristoteles cleverly shews in "Turba Philosophorum"; and Bernhardus in his "Practica" says: "The fount is to the king as a mother, whom she bears within herself, and kills him. But the king rises again, and becomes so strong that no man can wound him." Hence philosophers say: "Although the king is, before the world, more precious and worthy than Bega, yet alone can he bear no fruit." This Virgin and Blessed Water have philosophers in their books called by a thousand names, as a Heaven, Celestial Water, Heavenly Rain, Heavenly or May Dew, Water of Paradise, Aqua Regia, Corrosive Aqua Fortis, a sharp vinegar and brandy, a Quintessence of Wine, a waxy green juice, a waxy Mercury, a water becoming green, and

Green Lion, a Quicksilver, a Menstruum, a Blood and Menstruum, urine and horse-urine, Milk, and Virgin's Milk, white Arsenic, Silver, a moon and an humour of the moon, a woman and woman's seed, a sulphureous, steamy water and smoke, a fiery burning spirit, a mortal penetrating poison, a basilisk which kills everything, an envenomed worm, a poisonous snake, a dragon, a poisonous serpent which devours its offspring, a strong fire, and a clear $\triangle$, a fire of horse dung and horse dung, a sharp salt and sal armoniac, a saltary and common salt, a sharp soap, lye, and viscous oil, an ostrich-stomach which devours and digests an eagle, a vulture and hermetic bird, a seal and vessel of Hermes, a smelting and calcining stove. Innumerable other names of beasts, birds, vegetables, waters, humours, of milk, of blood, and of men have been given to it. Philosophers have spoken of it in their books, moreover, in a figurative manner, that such a ∇ should be made out of such things, and all the fools who have sought it in such things, have never found the desired water.

But, know this, my dearest son, that it is only made out of live Mercury, and from no other foreign thing in the world. The philosophers have given it these many names in order that the unwise may never know it. And you, my son, will have concluded the first part of this treatise, when you understand and know, that without this fire all the toil of the whole world and of alchemy is mere loss, and all alchemical processes are a delusion, unprofitable and false. For the Great Rosary says: "The receipt consists of only one thing, and with this key all the books of the philosophers are particularly and universally closed, and surrounded and guarded as with a strong wall. He who has not yet acquired the key can never enter the fortified castle, or obtain anything profitable. For this water is the one only key for opening the metallic walls. Further, this water is the strong aquafortis which Isaac refers to in his fragmentary work, and wherewith he dissolved bodies and made them spiritual. Therefore, diligently note, all alchemical work without this is only lies and falsity, whether metallic, mineral, vegetable, or animal substances are used. It is dissolved, sublimated, distilled, calcinated, extracted, mixed, compounded, as one will. One may dissolve it in cellars, in the bath, in dung, in aquafortis, and in all manner of strong waters, in every possible way, as the alchemical processes direct. We may make oil, water, lime, powder, black, white, yellow, and red. We may burn it, we may melt it in any possible fashion, even as the alchemical receipts tell us, and call it the true means for making gold and silver, yet from beginning to end it is abomination and falsity. I myself, with my own hands (for once I disbelieved this), have experienced such loss and damage.

Therefore, my son, be fully warned against the sophistry of Alchemy and all sophisticating, deceitful people. Beware of them as you would beware of the devil who works mischief. Avoid them as an impure, pitiless, and consuming fire, even as a deadly poison, for a man comes to destruction of both body and soul, honour and goods, through this sophistry and self-insinuating false Alchemy. It is worse than the devil himself, for it is possible to expend (the wealth of) a whole kingdom thereon; yet everything is destroyed, and no fundamental truth is found out. Accordingly, open your eyes. Recognise the only key; avoid falsity, for it is impossible in any other way to obtain anything true or profitable, save in that way which I have now shewn in this book.

A Short Admonition to the Reader.

I DO not personally know who the exceedingly propitious and beloved reader of the remarkable foregoing treatise may be, but I communicate what I have obtained to you, and would fain that the other portion of the small book were also forthcoming, and entirely printed. You will not, however, think that I withhold it from jealousy, as is the common case with others in their editions of such philosophical tracts. But because I have communicated to you the mercurial water and permanent water, wherein chiefly consists the key of this Art, and this has been done in a useful and faithful manner, I will give the further processes requisite in my other volume—*Thesaurinella Aurea Olympica Tripartita*, which will come out next

Easter, and will contain a collection of the writings of the Philosophers, printed for the first time, concerning the Blessed Stone of the Wise, so that you will have sufficient and useful instruction to your heart's desire, and will know how to thank me for it. When I get the other part I will not keep it from you. I have always wished and prayed to be the means of your instruction.

Farewell, with the love of God, which passes understanding!

Certain Verses of an Unknown Writer, concerning the Great Work of the Tincture.

Wilt thou, by God's grace alone.
Obtain the Stone of the Philosophers?
If so, seek it not in vegetables or animals,
In sulphur, quicksilver, and minerals;
Vitriol, alum, and salt are of no value;
Lead, tin, iron, and copper profit nothing;
Silver and gold have no efficacy.
Hyle or Chaos will accomplish it all.
It is enclosed in our salt spring,
In the tree of the Moon and of the Sun.
I call it the Flower of Honey,
The Flower known to the Wise.
In fine, the Flower and Honey
Are the Sulphur and Quicksilver of the Wise,
Even water and earth,
With the whitish seed of all metals.
The water is volatile, the earth fixed;

One can effect nothing without the other.
Both are born of a root having a white exterior.
It produces all the virtues of the metals,
Yet is it not dug from the ore
Either with pickaxes or other instruments.
In the place and spot where our Matter is found
No other metal whatever exists.
It is produced, with its virtue and efficacy,
In Hyle or Chaos alone.
Homer knew it well, and called it *Moly*.
This, in its proper condition,
Has a root altogether black.
It is green, white, and blood red.
The god Mercury offered it to Ulysses,
Even unto Ulysses in his wanderings,
As a precaution against the sorcery of Circe.
The gods also have bestowed it upon man
As a singularly great gift,
Designed to assuage and comfort him.
Hence springs pleasing nectar,

The drink of the goddesses.
It is also termed Chelidonia,
As a singular gift of Heaven.
Solar Root is another name.
The root is known to the wise:
It receives high honours in astronomy,
Is metaphorically likened to the planets,
Lead, tin, copper, and iron,
Silver and gold, everything the wise have named.
In the tongue of Chaldæa it is also called Azoth;
In German it is a blessed spirit;
In Latin, argent vive animate,
That is to say, Mercury of the Philosophers.
It is also named the herb *Adrop*,
A well-known Chaldæan word,
Signifying in our speech Saturn.
Astronomically speaking, I must say
That Saturn rules the earth.
Metaphorically is our matter compared,
Being the Red Lead and Red Earth,
With fools despised and valueless.
It is called the Red and Green Lion.
It is well known as the Adamic Earth—

A skilful production of the Wise Creator,
Which doth contain and unite in one mass
The powers of all natures.
From this mass and red earth,
Almighty God creates Adam.
He has highly honoured our first father,
Who is also called Microcosmus.
You are to recognise the Red Earth as Adam;
We call it the First Matter.
Later on, I will likewise disclose its preparation.
With great courage kill the lion;
But take its coagulated blood,
The brilliancy of gold and its costliness,
Separated from the centre of the putrefying earth;
Dissolve it with the greatest diligence;
Imitate the Creator of Nature so wise,
Who will vouchsafe to enlighten our understanding,
That we may separate the dry from the moist.
Thus water is produced from earth,
The volatile from the fixed,

The animated spirit on the earth.
Water and earth, two visible elements,
Have, by God's grace and care,
Fire and air concealed within them.
They are also purely impregnated
With the fifth invisible nature.
But, to proceed to the end of the work,
Marry the woman with the man,
Our Adam with clear Eve,
Both being absolutely naked,
For then Nature herself, being clean and pure,
Rejoices with her own nature.

The animated spirit dissolves the body,
The body coagulates the spirit.
This is the sole Mercury,
Which is the Foundation of the Stone of the Wise.
It becomes black, white, green, and red,
Is itself Proteus, the God of the sea,
Who, being caught, so wondrously
Transforms himself into a thousand shapes;
That is, it dissolves and coagulates itself,
Sublimates and calcines,

Mortifies and vivifies,
Washes and incerates,
Clarifies and fixes.
In all these things
Heaven and earth are concerned,
And the Sun and the Moon
Become dark and black as a raven:
Heaven and earth are melted quite away:
Truly, in the Hyle or Chaos
There is a most wonderful strife
Of the elements in all directions.
Water covers all the earth,
But, in order that the moist may become dry,
Our strong giants maintain
Incessant and unwearying contests
With our wondrously small dwarf,
Who, finally, by divine miracle,
Conquers and overcomes
And captures them all, both slays and binds.
Out of the destroyed rubbish
God creates a new Heaven and Earth.
The New Jerusalem is built
With transparent clear gold,

Also with pure precious stone.
Here is placed the famed Stone of the Wise,
The unique bird, the good Phœnix,
Who by the glow of the fire
Is slain and born again,
And becomes a real Salamander,
Who now lives in the fire.
This is *filius solis*, child of the sun,
Who with his singular power
Works miracles and great wonders,
And can expel all sicknesses
In human and metallic bodies.
With glorified body, flesh and blood,
He purifies all that is corporal.
The immortal Adam, highly endowed,
Tinges common gold and silver,
So that they thereby may become fruitful,
To bear their blessed likeness on the Earth.

ENIGMAS CONCERNING THE TINCTURE.

Question the First.
All things are compounded in triads;
They also rejoice in the number four,
Yet they resolve themselves into unity,
For otherwise nothing could exist.
It is indeed a subtle vapour,
And proceeds from Divine favour.
Tell me, then, what is this art?

First Answer.
A point which suddenly goes in a circle,
Wherein quadrant and triangle stand:
If you obtain it, you have the secret,
And escape poverty, want, and peril.

Question the Second.
I am sprung from four.
Your war harasses and slays me.
Could I but end this war,
Then my soul would never depart from me.
Your war destroys the green grass.
Alas for advice! what good does that?

Second Answer.

If you desire to unite the evil four,
That they may not depart from one another
Under the test of fire, then make them fire.
Thus you will possess a treasure richer far
Than Charles of Ghent could count,
Although he were a rich man.

Question the Third.

At first, there were four,
Yet now are there only three.
Before, there were five,
Yet release the fourth;
Otherwise we cannot use them.
Instruct me, what kind of being is this?

Third Answer.

One and four compose five completely,
But three and one make a bad four.
If you wish to reduce the three to unity,
And cannot, then make it nothing.

Question the Fourth.

Who is it, whose war is readily
But with secresy prepared?
Yet there cannot be war without warriors:
I need four of them for this strife.

Instruct me, now, where are there such
  people?

Fourth Answer.

From the green meadows
Come forth our giants;
From the deep mines
Proceed our dwarfs.
Vesuvius and Etna furnish us
With the children of the fire.
The deep waters produce our nymphs;
Our water is not disagreeable.
Instruct us what this is?

Final and Universal Rule.

On the Mount of Venus, on the green
  heath,
You will find your answer.
Seven companions go in and out,
Drinking with gusto a sour wine,
Ogling also a beautiful woman,
Whom they regard with looks of love.
This love befools their bodies,
So eagerly desire they the woman.
These men will expound thy questions,
And quickly answer the same.
Now cease thy questions,
For more I may not tell thee.

A Short Admonition to the True-Hearted Reader and Son of the Doctrine.

WELL-BELOVED Friend, Brother, and Reader, since this book is coming to an end, I have obtained the following description of the potable gold from my dear and most trusty friend, John George Cressius, citizen of Heidelburg, and lover of chemistry. He wishes me to append to it the statement that it is the work of Theophrastus. I cannot say for certain that it belongs to our dear Teacher, since many processes and writings appear among the lovers of Alchemy bearing his name, but such as he would never have thought of writing in such a fashion. However this may be, may it prove not unpleasing to thee that I place after it a remarkably instructive tract of Dom. Jacob Montanus, Doctor at Konigsburg, Prussia. The treatise deals with the efficacious administration of the glorious antidote called potable gold, the highly desirable, universal medicine for all diseases. Take this *Pandora* for the present, and be welcome to it. As to what may be wanting in it, I will send thee it in our "Olympic Golden Treasure," to be printed at Frankfort, as also in our "New Olympic Rosary," which, as an appendix to the "Golden Fleece," is to appear at Basle, if God will, this Easter. If I find that this work which I dedicate to thee is acceptable, thou wilt see next Michaelmas, and the following Easter, four or five additional tracts, by ancient and modern writers, concerning the Philosopher's Stone, if it be God's will, if it please thyself, and the publisher sufficiently remunerates me. Vale.

Concerning the Potable Gold of Theophrastus Paracelsus.

TAKE an old Hungarian wine which has not been drawn off, but still remains on its stand, and is already clear, the older the better, and extract its spirit. At first there goes up a little phlegm, and shews itself with streaks. When the rectified spirits ascend, no streaks are to be seen, and when these re-commence, and the evaporation leaves off, distil the spirit again, and leave a little behind; this is now phlegm. Repeat the process six or seven times, in each case leaving a little behind, until the spirits be quite separated from their phlegm.

Test for the Spirits.

Take a small and fine linen cloth, moisten it with any spirit, set fire to the cloth, and when it is completely consumed, the spirit of wine is rectified. Next, drop in a drop of olive oil, as the spirit falls from the stand to the bottom, and remains on the bottom, as fast as one stirs up; then you will have completely and rightly distilled the spirit of wine.

After this, take the extracted phlegm and distil it very slowly; at first a little spirit will evaporate; you may keep the same to drink; continue to distil the phlegm slowly, and there will remain at the bottom a beautiful white earth. Keep this, as also the phlegm; next, distil the remaining phlegm about two measures; keep the phlegm, for it will serve you for the first phlegm. Afterwards, completely distil the matter; a black substance will remain at the bottom, smelling as offensively as pitch, while the black matter is still moist. In order to pour it out, pour it into a retort and distil it very slowly, when phlegm will at first arise; throw this away, and when the oil begins to dissipate, put it out into another receptacle; distil the oil slowly, and carefully preserve it. After this, destroy the retort; take out the black matter; break it into pieces as large as beans; let a potter construct you a vessel shaped like a Wallenburgian box, with a lid; put the black earth therein; elutriate the box well, and let it dry. Place it in a fire, at first gentle, afterwards strong, for this purpose covered with coals. Let it remain in this condition twelve hours; then let the fire cool so that the matter may become cold. Afterwards, put it on again, and calcine it as at first. Then the matter will become beautifully white like paper; pound it small; pour upon it some of the phlegm which I gave instructions should be kept hot; let it stand four-and-twenty hours, when a salt will be extracted from the earth; pour it away from its dregs, and again pour another phlegm upon it; then let it stand twenty-four hours while more salt is being extracted Repeat the process till the extraction ceases. Then throw away the remaining earth, which looks like sand. After this, extract the phlegm, and a beautiful white salt will remain. Repeat the process six or seven times, so that it retains the moisture; otherwise it will not receive the spirit of wine.

Now, pour upon the salt a little spirit of wine; shake it well; pour it into a phial in such a way that the spirit of wine may pass over it to the breadth of two or three little fingers. Then let it stand two months putrefying, and the spirit of wine will acquire a beauteous red colour, and become even as an oil. After this, take as much gold from the gold beaters as you wish, put it in a phial, pour the spirit of life upon it, wherein its salt is dissolved; let it stand for about three months in a moderate heat, and the red will turn into a beautiful yellow, and will extract the soul of the sun into itself. Pour this away, distil it by means of the alembic, and the spirit of the sun will arise with the spirit of water, and will be potable medicine. Its salt will remain behind, which you may keep.

Of the Power, Operation, and Exceedingly Beneficial Use of the Glorious Antidote termed Potable Gold.

THE worthies of antiquity, before as well as after Christ, have, with the greatest diligence, laboured in most searching enquiry and investigation into the nature of and concerning the property and potent efficacy which reside deeply hidden in gold, which also innumerable writings on the subject serve to demonstrate.

Now, it is not without reason that their zeal has caused them to labour and toil so wearily, because they have seen that the greatest constancy of all God's earthly creations lies hidden in gold, which by no element can be destroyed or broken without extraordinary skill. All other creatures, as silver, precious stones, pearls, corals, spices, vegetables, and all kinds of herbs, howsoever named, although Divinely endowed every one with great power and virtue, cannot, notwitstanding, resist fire and the other elements, but yield and are destroyed.

In consequence, our ancient worthy men have made a commencement, and sought in many ways, and at great cost, wherewith, and by what means, the said noble creature of God might be compelled to yield its infinite power and virtue to succour human health, and become indisputably theirs. Many industrious investigators have diligently asked God for understanding, so as to arrive at the end they desire. Many, however, and the majority, have thought to force the sun by disgusting things, corrosive salt, urine, Mercury, and the like, but have accomplished nought, since, using, as aforesaid, noxious substances, they have prepared injurious medicines, which cannot be employed without harm and damage.

Thus, these unskilful workers, ignorant of the nature and property of this gold, can accomplish nothing, either by fire or any other way, and in consequence imagine that it is impossible to force the gold without the corrosives, and to reduce it to a potable gold.

Yet is it manifest that God Almighty has created all creatures in the water and on the earth solely for the use of man, and has appointed man as the ruler of them all. Hence it follows that there exists nothing so trifling and mean, but, applied externally or internally, it may be put to a medicinal use.

However, the noble metal and medicine is never, as many suppose, to be sought in acids; still less from other species of metals can it be extracted, even with the aid of fire, for it resists all this, but must be compelled by a special subtlety, and be changed from its first form and metallic nature. Afterwards its power and virtue are extracted by means of a pure, specially prepared spirit of wine, in the same way as noxious herbs, without the use of any corrosive whatever. The potable gold prepared with corrosives cannot be used without great harm and damage.

As to how, and in what manner, the sages thought that gold could be compelled to yield its power and virtue, a thing most people deem impossible, I ought to reveal to every considerate man, though, notwithstanding, little thanks will be gained, even when I have appealed to the uprightness of my life, and though the expenses I have incurred should be considered. I have no hesitation whatever to point it out, and thereby openly dissipate all suspicion. Consequently, I have, as soon as possible, made a short relation concerning the preparation, whereby anyone may know for whom this, my already prepared Potable Gold, may be used, in that it is prepared without any corrosive matter, and can be used with no risk whatever as a universal medicine in all serious maladies.

Know, in the first place, that before the medicine can be properly used in long-standing sicknesses and weaknesses, it is necessary that the body be purified by proper medicines, as a learned and skilful physician directs. For with regard to sudden dangerous sickness, as apoplexy, epilepsy, cordialgia, syncope, *tremor cordis*, and the like, it is permissible to use the tincture at once; yet in the case of such severe dangerous illnesses, when the attack itself is allayed, it is well, before further employment of this tincture of gold, that the body be none the less previously purified.

In the next place, we must be careful concerning the amount of the dose, to avoid administering too much or too little; it is beneficial to give a full-grown adult eight *guttæ*, or small drops. A person half-grown takes five or six; a child but one drop. The distilled water or wine that accompanies the dose must not exceed a single spoonful.

In the third place, in the case of chronic sicknesses, it should be taken daily, early in the morning and about five or six at night, after four or five hours fasting. When necessity requires, and the sickness has obtained a firm hold, it may be used thrice a day, that is to say, in the morning, between the two meals, two hours before dinner, and in the evening, two hours after supper. If the patient wishes to sleep, no further meal must be taken for two hours. This daily use must be kept up eight or fourteen days, according to the nature of the disease.

In the fourth place, it is necessary that potable gold be taken with things appropriate to it. We must regard the qualities, effects, and position of the same; for this reason, various accompaniments are suitable. It must be used to allay pain of a headache with water of betony. In case of giddiness, balm is necessary Insomnia requires *aqua vitæ*, betony, or marjoram ▽. Apoplexy requires water with extract of lavender; also place separately two or three drops at first on the tongue. The same quantity is used for paralysis. For a bad memory use a decoction of the roots of fennel and acorns.

Melancholy, sadness, and similar emotions of the mind, which are especially seated in the head, require betony and pæony water, together with the potable gold, or liquor of oak mistletoe, but never anything hot, for this fills and oppresses the head. Should the malady arise from feverish blood, use water of common fumitory. Borrage water dissipates and wards off all weakness and feebleness of the head, and preserves the constitution.

In epilepsy, or falling sickness, the potable gold must be used with pæony water, or with a decoction of the root of pæony, collected while the moon wanes; in the case of an old or full-grown man, at the beginning of the paroxysm. The same is required when the paroxysm has ceased. A child of a year or eighteen months, and of corresponding size, must be given one drop. A very young child must, at the commencement, middle, and end of the attack, only have the point of its tongue smeared by means of a piece of wood dipped in olive oil. Continue the application till the epilepsy ceases altogether. In cases of ophthalmia, or abscess in the eye, use fennel, swallow-wort, or xerophthalmia water. For catarrh and rheum add violet root water. For toothache drop a little into the tooth. For bleeding of the nose, scabious or plantain water must be used. For phthisis or consumption use honey water or milk. For ulcer of the lungs, take water wherein crabs have been caught, well corrected. For offensive breath, orthopnœa, and other cold and rheumy diseases, use water of Marrubius, hyssop, fennel, and the like. In cases of trembling or palpitating of the heart, use balm or borrage water. With pains of the stomach use balm mint water, or a decoction of balm mint.

In fainting or heaviness place one or two drops on the tongue, with borrage or sorrel water. For the iliac passion, or twisting of the guts, use plantain water. For the worm use a decoction of zedoary. In costiveness, pain or swelling of the liver, or dropsy, where external heat is the cause, use plantain or liverwort water. When the illness is occasioned by cold, use a decoction of spikenard and of cinnamon, for it removes the obstruction. In costiveness of the spleen use ash-tree water. In melancholy the potable gold must be administered with temperate, not with cold or hot, things, but with fumitory water, young hops, or nettlemoth water, or with *liquor cornucervus*, also with rose sugar, syrup of betony, after a slight purgation of the melancholy and morbid humour has been effected by the syrup of epithimum and cichorium, which humour produces the obstruction. Otherwise, the virtues of this potable gold would be extinguished and frustrated. This must also be understood of other medicinal extracts. For pain in the stones and the kidneys, use aquatic nut water, radish water, pimpernel water, or philanthropist's powder. In case of strangury or injury to the reins, employ fresh goat's milk. With rupture use a species of woundwort or common comfrey water. In obstruction or retention of the menstrual courses, taking place not only in the matrix but in all other parts of the body whence the matrix receives its nourishment, the channels which convey nourishment are choked up. Since there is no nutriment in the uterus, there is also no menstruous excrement, and alarming symptoms supervene. The potable gold, however, is most excellent in removing this evil, wine mixed with herbs being employed for a week, twice or thrice daily, early in the morning, and at night, about four or five drops being used at a time. It is a marvellous secret in the case of any menstrual flow, ensuring proper regularity. Women take it, as Theophrastus and others witness, even when fifty or sixty. Moreover, because the potable gold sets right the flow of the white and red, not restraining it like the ordinary astringents, but separating the bad from the good, it assists Nature to expel the bad, retaining what is good for the nourishment of the uterus; it is utilized in suffocation of the uterus, as the case requires, with wormwood water, orange peel water, endive, wormwood, salt, etc. The potable gold is also used with wormwood in cases of difficult birth. For sterility, water of Neptune or lavender is required. In cases of gout of the foot or the hand, burning water, or water of paralysis, or lavender water, is necessary.

When there is plague, it is good, if the malady and falling sickness permit, previously to administer a lenitive of cassia, manna, and the like, according as one ascertains from the symptoms what humour has infected the body and rules it, afterwards employing the potable gold with other purgatives. In cases of putrid fever, arising from humours, as takes place in a mild pestilence, antiseptics must be taken. When the putrefaction abounds in humours, then the appropriate lenitives must be used, but nothing acid. These humours must be dealt with in this manner since they would hinder the operation of the potable gold. Various accidents originate them. We have here given the best instruction how the poison may be warded off, either by perspiration or vomit. Therefore this potable gold is in this case used with lemon water, liquor of Carduus Benedictus, sandal wood, stag's head, syrup from the acidity of lemons, with water of citron, conserve of roses, of borrage, water germander, in cases of heated paroxysms and with a warm condition of the body, etc. But if the heat were moderate, and the poison were situated in cold humour, it would be properly administered with theriacal water of pimpernel, vervain, angelica, and pomegranate. Moreover, pearls, corals, and salt of absinth may be added.

In the case of gangrene, fistula, itches, the potable gold with *aqua pedis Columbini* and sorrel water, externally and internally used, has healing efficacy. As for poison, it preserves those who are poisoned or bitten by a mad dog. It cures them with white tormentil or snake's root water.

The gold must be administered in the case of quartan and other fevers with water of Capones, theriacal water, water of Carduus Benedictus, or a sufficient decoction of the root of fennel, pimpernel, and salt of absinth. It is generally given at the commencement of the paroxysm. Perspiration must, if possible, follow.

In certain complaints of the belly we require water of the dodder of thyme, fumitory water, with liquor in water Garyophyllorum Maris, with a decoction of Vincitoxicus and of Chamædius, with a syrup of the acidity or the juice of lemons. Finally, it may be used against all maladies which are formally named by physicians. Yet we must be careful that, together with these sicknesses, we take into consideration the other indispositions or diseases which humours originate, as when, for instance, heat and cold are present, that we may know the opportunity for using a suitable preparation. Thus the potable gold is powerfully conducive to preservation and cure in the case of miners, assayers, alchemists, goldsmiths, cannon founders, mint-wardens, and all those who have been poisoned with poisonous smoke, and especially with mercury sublimate, crude and precipitate, or however it may be termed.

It is especially efficacious with those whose constitutions have been ruined by grease and fumes from the precipitate, and such matters. In this case the gold is accompanied with treacle water, scabious water, water of pimpernel, *anthos* with the sap of the holy wood, horn of stag, rhubarb, Muscat nuts, *conserva anthos*, syrup from the juice of lemons, bark of citron, of Mithridates, etc. We must also add, if necessary, the redness of pomegranate, and the pearl salt of absinth.

Finally, this potable gold destroys all superfluous moisture in the body; when rightly used, externally and internally, it expels all impurities, is an excellent purgative of every poison, purifies the blood, not by evacuation, but passing imperceptibly through all the limbs, renews them, retains that which is good, expelling the bad, being the true tincture of the wise, for consuming the remains of diseases, and increasing the natural heat of the body, surpassing herein all other medicaments. It is also efficaciously employed for fistulas, gangrenes, and all incurable ulcers, externally applied. This potable gold is also used with wine for leprosy. So much for the present concerning the right use of this glorious antidote. Should further information on this subject be desired, it can be obtained by consulting me at my house.

JACOB MONTANUS,

Doctor of Medicine at Konigsburg, in Prussia, in the year of our Lord, 1595.

FINIS.

INDEX.

Adam, and Adam of Philosophers, 10, 34, 37, 70, 100, 160, 220, 232, 256, 257, 329.
Adrop, 329.
Alanus, 308, 309.
Alcohoph, 42.
Aliocosoph, 42.
Alum, 260.
Aqua Vitæ, 269, 271, 276, 280, 292, 293, 297.
Aristotle, 35, 58, 309.
Arnoldus de Villa Nova, 303, 309, 313.
Art of Water, 161, 163.
Art of Separation, 162.
Astral Man, 110.
Astrum, 300.
Aurelius Augurellus, 206, 212, 225, 230, 241, 253.
Avicenna, 37, 47, 50, 51, 54.
Azoth, 42, 259, 329.

Basil Valentine, 26.
Bernhardus, 201, 217, 220, 223, 231, 234, 240, 242, 243, 248, 249, 263, 320.
Bodies—The Two Bodies in Man, 17.
Books of the Magi, 171, *et seq.*

Calcination, 288.
Calid, 223, 230.

Ceration, 289.
Christ, a Spagyric Philosopher, 13.
Cœlum Philosophicum, 275, 280.
Conjunction, 226.
Cornelius Agrippa, 203.
Cressius, J. G., 337.

Dissolution, 295.
Distillation and Extraction, 222.
Divine Magic, 12.

Eagle of the Philosophers, 198, 205, 207, 208, 249, 261, 262.
Elixir of Life, 40.
Euclides, 303.
Everlasting Balsam, 213.
Exaltation, 246.

Fermentation, 246.
Ferment of Metals, 255.
Ferrariensis, 209, 215.
Fifth Essence, 34, 35, *et seq.*, 54, 55, 60, 61, 73, 74, 85, 222, 259, 297, 313.
Filius Solis, 333.
First Matter, 162, 199, *et seq.*, 224.
Four Elements, 34, 78.
Fumus Salis, 117.
Fusible Gold, 276.

Galenus, 93, 97.
Geber, 225.
Generation of Metals, 80, *et seq.*
Gold—Extraction of, 1; Generation of, 81; Common, 82; Conversion into, 86; and Mercury, 282; as a Ferment, 284; see also 82, 85, 86, 92, 93, 139, 145, 151, 155, 252, 276, 279, 280, 282, 283, 284, 285, 286, 290, 291, 294, 296, 300, 343, *et seq.*
Golden Fleece, 76.
Grand Secret, 278, 285.
Great Work, 294.

Heaven—the two Heavens in Man, 24.
Hermes, 33, 35, 100, 195, 197, 199, 200, 209, 228, 239, 251, 321.
Humor Lunæ, 206.
Hyle, 327, 332.

Ignis non Urens, 153.
Iliastic Heaven, 24.
Incineration, 269.
Inner Man, 110, 130.
Isaac the Philosopher, 8, 301.

Kybrick, 42.

Laton, 287.
Leo Suavius, 140.
Lion of Philosophers, 198, *et seq.*, 207, 208, 211, 216, 217, 218, 219, 221, 222, 228, 233, 249, 261, 262, 329.

Little Summer, 236.
Liquor Lunæ, 297, 304.
Luna, 284, 285; Luna Cerebrum, 24; Lime of Silver, 280; Luna Metaphorica, 304.

Macrocosmus, 23, 161, *et seq.*, 186, 194, 196.
Magnesia, 259, 264.
Medicine of Philosophers, 8, 25, 68, *et seq.*, 76, 169, 184, 185, 251, 266, 289, 292.
Menstruum, 288, 307.
Mercury and Quicksilver, 131, 132, 139, 142, 143, 146, 147-157, 198, 213, 218, 229, 238, 250, 255, 257, 259, 266, 267, 269, 274, 275, 277, *et seq.*, 304, 305, 311, 312, 316-318, 344.
Mercurial Salt, 158.
Microcosmus, 23, 161, 186, 194, 233, 252.
Moly, 328
Morienus, 36, 47, 118, 194, 201, 229, 309.
Mortification, 277.
Mulciber, 2.

Natural Revelation, 9.
Natural Mysteries, 13.
Nature, Books of, 20, 21, 22; Secrets of, 55.
New Birth, 158.

One Subject, 85.
One Thing, 34, 35.

Paracelsus, 8, 9, 21, 26-29, 89, 91-96, 99, 105, 106, 108-110, 112-114, 117, 121, 123, 124, 128-131, 136-143, 145-150, 153, 156, 194, 202, 209, 214, 221, 226, 227, 229, 249, 252, 256.
Philosopher's Heaven, 275.
Philosophical Seed, 235.
Philosophy—Three kinds, 5; the Heavenly and Eternal, 19; the Mortal and Natural, 20.
Physica Tinctura, 276.
Primum Mobile, 58.
Putrefaction, 285.

Raphael, 43.
Raven's Head, 232.
Raymund Lully, 213, 235, 308, 310, 311, 312.
Rebis, 266.
Red Spirit, 315.
Red Tincture, 281.
Richard the Englishman, 203, 218, 300, 301.

Sal Alpoli, 273.
Salt, 120, 134, 142, 157, 158, 166, 179, 198, 213, 238, 267, 269, 271, *et seq.*, 317, 318, 327, 344.
Sandaraca, 42.
Seed of Metals, 79, 81, 253, 327.
Seven Liberal Arts, 44.
Solution, 279.
Soul of the World, 37, 72, 75, 76, 206, 210, 230.

Souls — the Eternal and the Natural, 24.
Spagyric Philosophy, 15, 21.
Spirit of the World, 53, 59, 61, 62, 72, 75.
Stars—their Influence and Instruction, 16; how to overcome, 19; Magnet of, 23; of Paracelsus, 110, 112; 119, 137.
Stone of the Philosophers, 8, 25, 30, 45, 75, 87, 237, 238, 239, 255, 267, 277, 280, 291, 316.
Sulphur of Iron, 277.
Sulphur of Gold, 277.
Sulphur, 120, 134, 155, 166, 198, 217, 218, 255, 257, 266, 267, 278, 279, 281, *et seq.*, 301, 327.
Sun and Moon, 52, 53, 54, 55, 62, 63, 64, 66, 68, 114, 152, 184, 185, 187, 252, 269, 285, 296, 299, 302.

Tartar, 89, 91, 114-120, 123-130, 132.
Tartarus Auri, 139.
Turba Philosophorum, 240, 248, 298, 309, 320.

Venus, 282.
Vitriol, 89, 91, 138.

Water, 73, 161, 163, 164, 166, 171, 177, 179, 186, 204, 205, 215, 217, 218, 225, 228, 231, 233, 237, 246, 259, 266, 299, 304, 305, 307, 309, 312, 313, 319, 320, *et seq.*